POSTS

SUNY Series in Postmodern Culture
Edited by Joseph Natoli

POSTS

Re Addressing the Ethical

Dawne McCance

STATE UNIVERSITY OF NEW YORK PRESS

Published by
State University of New York Press, Albany

For information, address State University of New York Press,
State University Plaza, Albany, N.Y., 12246

Production by Cathleen Collins
Marketing by Theresa Abad Swierzowski

The following publishers have generously given permission to use extended quotations from copyrighted works. From "Sensus communis: the subject in *statu nascendi*," trans. M. Hobson and G. Bennington, *Paragraph* vol. 11, no. 1, © 1988 Oxford University Press, reprinted by permission of Oxford University Press. From "Deconstruction and the other," in *Dialogues With Contemporary Continental Thinkers* by Richard Kearney, © 1984 Manchester University Press. From "Viability and the Use of the Fetus," by H. Tristram Engelhardt, in *Abortion and the Status of the Fetus*, ed. William Bondeson, H. T. Engelhardt, Stuart Spicker, and Daniel Winship, © 1983 Kluwer Academic Publishers, reprinted by permission of Kluwer Academic Publishers. From "Difference," by Stephen Heath, *Screen* 19, 1978. From "Postmodernism, or the Cultural Logic of Late Capitalism," by Frederic Jameson in *The New Left Review* 146, © 1984. From "Women's Time," by Julia Kristeva, trans. Alice Jardine and Harry Blake, in *Signs* 7.1, © 1981 by The University of Chicago Press, reprinted by permission of the publisher. From "Women in the Beehive: A Seminar With Jacques Derrida," in *Men in Feminism*, ed. Alice Jardine and Paul Smith, © 1987 Methuen & Co. From *Languages of the Unsayable* by Sanford Budick and Wolfgang Iser, © 1989 by Columbia University Press, reprinted with permission of the publisher. From *The Possessed Individual* by Arthur Kroker, published by New World Perspectives, © 1992 Arthur Kroker. From "Ethics and the postmodern Imagination," by Richard Kearney in *Thought* 62, © 1987 Fordham University Press, reprinted by permission of the publisher. From "Passions: 'An Oblique Offering'," by Derrida, trans. Davin Wood in *Derrida: A Critical Reader*, ed. David Wood, © 1992 Blackwell Publishers. From "Love Me, Love My Ombre, Elle," by Gayatri Chakravorty Spivak in *Diacritics*, © 1984 The Johns Hopkins University Press. From *The Differend* by Jean-François Lyotard, trans. George Van Den Alleele, © 1988 by the University of Minnesota, originally published as *Le Différend* © 1983 by Les Éditions de Minuit. From *The History of Sexuality* by Michel Foucault, trans Robert Hurley, © 1990 by Vintage Books. From "Feminism and Postmodernism," by Susan Rubin Suleiman in *Zeitgeist in Babel* ed Ingeborg Hoesterey, © 1991 Indiana University Press. From "Foucault's Discourse," by Hayden White in *The Content of Form*, © 1987 The John's Hopkins University Press.

Library of Congress Cataloging in Publication Data

McCance, Dawne, 1944-
    Posts : re addressing the ethical / Dawne McCance.
      p.   cm. — (SUNY series in postmodern culture)
    Includes bibliographical references and index.
    ISBN 0-7914-3001-4 (alk. paper). — ISBN 0-7914-3002-2 (pbk.: alk. paper)
    1. Ethics, Modern—20th century. 2. Postmodernism. I. Title.
II. Series.
BJ319.M36 1996
170'.9'04—dc20   95-33677
                                    CIP

10 9 8 7 6 5 4 3 2 1

*Thank you Robert Kroetsch, David Arnason,
Cassandra Devenney, Margaret Sweatman,
Erin McCance, Rob Merello.*

This book is for my mother and my father.

Contents

possible [F *possible*, L *possibilis*, f. *posse*, to be able, have power; *posse comitatus*, armed force or band of constables (OED: "the body of men above the age of fifteen in a county (exclusive of peers, clergymen, and infirm persons), whom the sheriff may summon or 'raise' to repress a riot or for other purposes . . . as in TRISTRAM *Gt. Sahara* x.160: 'On a house-top were a bevy of nut-brown maids, who . . . had forgotten to veil their faces. They were consequently pelted with stones by some of the *posse comitatus*, and retired in confusion.'")]: that can or may be; that may or can exist, be done, or happen; that is in one's power. Hence **potent** [L *potent*, *potens*, prp. of *potere*, *posse*, mighty, able, powerful, influential; deadly, that can kill; *potenter*, strongly, mightily; *potentia*, power, mastery, force, the rule of an individual; the ability to have an erection and sexual intercourse; *possideo*, hold possession of by power, hold by a title, be owner of; occupy, abide in a place; *possido* (*pot* of *potis* + *sido*), to take possession of, to possess one's self of, seize; (the base *pot-* is repr. also by Sk *pati*, lord, possessor, husband; and G *pósis*, spouse)]: powerful, able, virile; and **potentate** [L *potentatus*, might, power, dominion, control; a position of power and authority; *potentator*, a ruler, potentate]: power, rule, authority; a ruler, a man having great power or occupying a powerful position. So, **position** [L *pono*, *ponere*, to place, set, put; to post (military forces); to erect, set up; to lay to rest, put in a tomb, bury; to ordain, lay down a rule, definition, position, e.g., in speech or writing; *positio*, the action of placing, the place occupied by a person or thing, a place from which a view is taken; *positus*, position, site]: a putting, placing; the action of positing; the laying down of a proposition or thesis; a proposition or thesis laid down; the act of placing in a particular order or arrangement; a military site chosen for occupation by an army; place in the social scale; the place which one occupies in relation to an other; and **post** [L *postis*, a beam, door-post]: a stout timber, pillar, support; [L *post*, after, behind]: relating to time or order as in after, afterward, coming after; of local position; behind, posteriorly, following; the Latin preposition may occur in combination forms used in English contexts as in *postmortem*; performed or occurring after (some [one's]) death; *postpone*, to avoid, delay, defer; to place after; and *postscript*, written after the signature; [F *poste*, station, stand, It *posta*, post station, L *posta*, *postus*, *postum*, *positus*, *positum*, f. *pono*, *ponere*, to place]: an act of placing or posting; an entry in a ledger; that which is put or placed; a place where a soldier is stationed; name of a game, a stake in any game; a bugle call giving solemn notice, as in the *last post*; an act of placing or posting: one who travels with messages from post to post, an express messenger riding post, a courier, a postman, the bearer of a message; a dispatch, a relay; a medium used for conveyance of the mail, a postal network.

you under-
stand, within every sign already, every mark or every trait,
there is distancing, the post, what there has to be so that it is
legible for another, another than you or me

Derrida, *The Post Card*

Introduction

ON POSTMODERNISM AND THE
IMPOSSIBILITY OF ETHICS

> *Watch out, don't go too fast*
> > Derrida, "No Apocalypse, Not Now"
>
> *To go fast is to forget fast.*
> > Lyotard, *The Inhuman*
>
> *Don't go too fast.*
> > Lacan, *Le Séminaire XX, Encore*

> *Not impossible but* the *impossible. The very figure of the*
> *impossible. It announces itself, gives itself to be thought as*
> *the impossible. It is proposed that we begin by this.*
> > Derrida, *Given Time: 1. Counterfeit Money*

To begin is impossible. I will begin with that, with *postmodernism* as a figure of the impossibility of beginning, of positing (*posting*) a definition, a place, point or position from which to depart. What I will attempt in this Introduction is a brief overview of the work of five critics for whom definition *is* the point of departure, critics who (in advance, it seems, of reading the texts they critique) define what postmodernism is. My suggestion will be that by beginning with definition, and with postmodernism already defined, these critics designate, even before setting out, the destination at which they will arrive. It's as if they didn't begin after all.

Four of the critics whose postmodernisms I survey in this Introduction—Arthur Kroker, Fredric Jameson, Susan Rubin Suleiman and Linda

Hutcheon—are recognized theorists of the term. They are writers who have defined postmodernism for us, and whose definitions of the term have contributed significantly to the prominence of their work. The fifth critic, Alasdair MacIntyre, belongs less obviously to the group, since he does not define postmodernism explicitly and does not elaborate on others' definitions of it. I include him, however, as one whose work powerfully, if only implicitly, delimits the term. I include him as well because this delimitation provides the confine into which MacIntyre reads "the French."[1] My argument is that each of the five postmodernisms with which I begin is assimilative of the "French" writers whose work is the subject of the subsequent chapters of this book: Jacques Derrida, Jean-François Lyotard, Jacques Lacan, Julia Kristeva, Michel Foucault. Each of the North American critics I consider appropriates "the French" as exemplifying what postmodernism is.

A dubious exemplarity, I will suggest, this demarcating of "the French" within North American theoretical-institutional boundaries, and this for a number of reasons that I will consider in passing. For one thing, it collapses the heterogeneity in the writing of Derrida, Lyotard, Lacan, Kristeva and Foucault, as well as the differences of these writers one from the other. For another thing, it overlooks their resistance to "postmodernism" and all such periodizing terms. But perhaps most significantly for the question of ethics that interests me in this book, this demarcation of "the French" (mis)reads their work into a nostalgic rhetoric of impossibility. According to their North American critics, "the French" not only model postmodernism, they model where it goes wrong; they show us how and why postmodernism is ethically bankrupt; they leave us waiting for the post-postmodern. And what comes *after* postmodernism, these North American critics suggest, must be a return to what was *before*: to a subject and a project, to ethics as a discourse of possibility. It's as if "the ethical," thought otherwise, were missing altogether from the work of "the French." But this is a matter I will leave for the following essays, which take up the question of ethics in the writing of Derrida, Lyotard, Lacan, Kristeva and Foucault. For now, and by way of an Introduction, I turn to some of their critics.

The Last Post

To gaze upon René Magritte's painting *The False Mirror* is, according to Arthur Kroker, to be given a "a despairing, visual expression" (Kroker and Cook 1986, 79) of the void at the centre of postmodern experience. For the painting depicts a disembodied floating eye, that Kroker takes to be a figure of the postmodern body cut off from its surroundings and emptied of its own corporeality—"a scandal of absence" (80). What is postmodern about the Magritte painting, Kroker says, is this depiction of absence, the absence of possibility. Postmodernism is this: "not the presence—of terror, of filiations, of bodies, of embodiment—but the precise *absence* of possibility: the absence of ontology, sensuous experience, and freedom" (84).

If Kroker privileges artistic work in *The Postmodern Scene* (1986), he privileges it as an aesthetic mirror, an "exact visual analogue" (282), of the nihilism of Western culture. That nihilism began in the fourth century with Augustine of Hippo, whose *De Trinitate* marked a turn away from corporeality that would reach its end-point only in the twentieth century, in the (disappearing) society of postmodern America. In *The Postmodern Scene*, as in Kroker's 1987 essay, "Panic Value," material bodies are said to have long since disappeared, to have *imploded* into "postmodern bodies as X-rayed afterimages" (1987, 192).[2] Thus Kroker reads Francesca Woodman's photographs of the body as presenting "a suicided vision of the postmodern kind" (Kroker and Cook 1986, 243), "a woman's vision of the taking of the flesh by the signs of dead power" (244). Woodman's photography makes of her body "a mirror of domination" (243), and the photographic image, in turn, reflects the fate of the postmodern body. Edward Hopper's paintings present a "searing vision of postmodernism as excremental culture" (252), a reflection of "what is happening to us on the inside as we are processed through the designed world of the technological system" (251). The art of Francis Bacon and Alec Colville reflects "a time of cluster suicides, cultural dyslexia and forms of schizophrenia, as the postmodern mind runs down to random disorganization and burnout, where hermetic bodies and schizoid egos become panic sites at the *fin-de-millennium*" (Kroker 1987, 193). And because his "vision of excess matches perfectly the popular mood of an American (and thus world) culture on the downside" (Kroker and Cook 1986, 280), Eric Fischl is "the quintessential artist of postmodern America" (281).

In 1984, in *Technology and the Canadian Mind*, Kroker could speak of "the objective conditions for a new, universal human culture" on the other side of the technological experience: technology as "just dangerous enough" to force "a dramatic revaluation of human ethics" (126). In 1985, in "The Phallocentric Mood: 'bored but hyper'," co-written with

Marilouise Kroker, he could say that feminism offers the possibility of such a recovery: "it's just like Magritte's brilliant depiction of blood from the head as rupture and transgression. *Memory*: that's the radical promise of feminist critique which is, against the global, cultural amnesia of the modern century, the historical remembrance of *temps perdu* and of better possibilities not yet achieved" (6). But by 1986 and *The Postmodern Scene*, Kroker's sense of the possibility of remembering the social, of "calling back to feminism as a universal politics" (Kroker and Kroker 1985, 6), has been displaced by descriptions of the postmodern "panic" mood: as in the medical-moral discourse on AIDS, where the defensive closing off of the body and hysteria over clean body fluids, are said to indicate a deep and radical anxiety over the collapse of the body social (see Kroker and Cook 1986, 13). Again in 1987, "a generalized panic fear about the breakdown of the immunological systems of American society" (Kroker and Kroker 1987, 12) characterizes postmodern culture. Postmodernism becomes "a melancholy descent into the violence of the death of the social" (Kroker and Cook 1986, 9); its scene, "the dead scene of the social" (Kroker and Kroker 1987, 15); its mood, a "generalized panic fear about the breakdown of the technological immunity systems of society as a whole" (12–13); a "deep sense of melancholia and a recognition of the loss of solidarity" (Kroker and Cook 1986, 13).

The lament continues when Kroker considers the work of "the French." Apparently unaware of Derrida's analysis of techno-criticism as thought thinking itself as a "thought of the essence,"[3] Kroker in *The Postmodern Scene* not only reconstitutes this very form of techno-critique but also reads Derrida into it. Postmodernism is said to be the "historical moment" (15) when technology triumphs in an all-encompassing "dead" power, a one-dimensional power that consumes "Derrida's *écriture*" (27). This power, similarly, renders obsolete Kristeva's attempt to theorize somatic difference. The tension between the semiotic and the thetic has already disappeared, Kroker says, "has already been absorbed by promotional culture" (23). Here, "the French" have come too late. Their effort is futile. Either that or, as Kroker also suggests in *The Postmodern Scene*, "French" writing provides, as does the Magritte painting, a cynical mirror of the technological triumph that postmodernism is. Thus Lacan: unlike Kristeva, Kroker suggests, Lacan acquiesced to the closure of postmodern technology. For Lacan's mirror stage is the account of a subject whose materiality has dissolved into a specular image, and Lacan's elevation of the signifier, "the bourgeois kingdom of the *I, Me, or Mine* sliding along the 'chain of signifiers' " (25) indicates that, along with materiality, meaning too is lost. But in *The Postmodern Scene*, the preeminent reflection of postmodern closure might be the work of Foucault, whose discourse on power Kroker reads as "a nominalism that is bleak with despair" (218).

Kroker's more recent book, *The Possessed Individual: Technology and the French Postmodern* (1992), again presents "the French mind" as cynical model or mirror, "a mirror of technology in the postmodern scene" (2). "The French" *reflect* the state of contemporary American culture, Kroker says. They are "fractal thinkers in whose central images one finds the key power configurations of the American hologram" (1). They excel at describing "the aftermath of the implosion of the technological dynamo as the language of mastery of social and non-social nature" (13). They give us to witness the triumph of *the virtual*, "the death of politics, the death of aesthetics, the death of the self, the death of the social, the death of sex" (13). Why study "the French"? Their texts are *panic sites*. They give us, as no others can, "a grisly but seductive description of possessed individualism in the terminal phase" (13).

In this book Kroker protrays the postmodern subject not as a consumer, not as liberalism's possessive individual, but as a possessed individual, the individual "as itself an object of consumption" (6). The possessed individual, whose corporeality has been consumed by the technological system, exists only as a *virtual* body, as the "after-image of a colonizing power" (157). Kroker reads Lyotard into this apocalyptic narrative: "he is a crash theorist" whose "writings evoke a culture in ruins" (141). Lyotard is "a brilliant example of Kant in ruins, of the disappearance of Kant's *Critique of Judgement* into virtual subjectivity" (146). And the importance of art in Lyotard's work is "as a model of how power functions in culture and society" (147). For Kroker, "Lyotard's world *actually* begins with the construction of subjectivity by the norms of technology" and his vision provides "an almost medical diagnosis of the human condition under the sign of liquid technology" (150).

But again, Kroker privileges Foucault. *The Possessed Individual* gives its last words to the "panic medicine" of *Birth of the Clinic*, the "panic madness" of *Madness and Civilization*, the "panic power" of *Discipline and Punish*, and especially, the "panic erotics" of the history of sexuality series—which, Kroker suggests, gave rise to the cynical (homo)sexuality of the *Panic Foucault*. Kroker describes *Panic Foucault* as "a thinker whose particular brilliance is that he actually became what he sought to describe" (161). Foucault ended his life with *The Use of Pleasure* and *The Care of the Self*, "texts about panic erotics: that moment when the body disappears into an empty sign, interpellated by all the ideologies, tattooed by the pleasures of a fully aestheticized sexuality, and inscribed by the languages of medicine, philosophy, and *oneiroheureutics*" (160). By concluding his last book and at the same time ending his life, "bleakly by noting the sterility of the philosopher's virtue for 'boys loving boys' " (162), Foucault demonstrated how "the game of the intellectual imagination, of life and death" (163) is played postmodern.

But I am wrong to say that *The Possessed Individual* gives its last words to Foucault. It closes with a two-page epilogue in which Kroker suggests that "the specific appeal of the French discourse on technology is a deeply ethical one" (165). For what this discourse provides is a theoretical vocabulary "for listening intently to the 'intimations of deprival' in the midst of the celebratory ruins of the American way" (165). Kroker is borrowing from George Grant here. His description of "the French mind" as "disclosing" or "reflecting" an American bourgeois subjectivity which has disappeared into virtual reality, matches his 1984 reading of Grant as "the Nietzsche of the New World," a Nietzsche whose writing laments the tragic penetration of technique, the will to mastery, into the deepest interstices of the American self. In *Technology and the Canadian Mind*, Kroker argues that Grant's work provides no exit from the darkness of this century but that, insofar as it shows us our "intimations of deprival," shows us that "*technique is ourselves*," it gives us at least a way of "living critically" in the present (28–31). And such, it seems, is Kroker's reading of "contemporary French thought": it emanates from beyond America's borders; is incapable of providing a way out of the darkness; but is "critical" nonetheless because it takes as its task the cynical mirroring of the technically constituted American self. What Kroker calls "the French mind" serves as "a reflection from beyond its dynamic horizon of the *virus* of technology in the empire of the American postmodern" (1992, 166). As though "the French mind" could do no more than offer itself as an *after-image*, as "a theoretical autobiography" (166), of Virtual America.

A Poetics of the Possible

In Jean Baudrillard's works, "the fatal disintegration of the West is arrayed in all of its melancholy excess," Kroker claims. "In his theoretical imagination are rehearsed all the main lines of a great, epochal, historical drama" (1992, 57). The drama in question records the passage from the age of the sign and referential signification to the era of the simulacrum and simulation. What happened, Baudrillard says, is "that the acceleration of modernity with respect to technology . . . brought us to an escape velocity such that one day we escaped the referential sphere of the real and of history" (1986, 18). The referential orbit was permanently broken and we entered the age of simulation, where it is as impossible to discover the real, as it is impossible to stage an illusion, because the real no longer exists (Baudrillard 1984, 266–67). It is impossible to do more than simulate; and yet to simulate is precisely "to feign to have what one hasn't" (254), to substitute signs of the real for the real that is no longer there— so as to leave the reality principle intact.

Alasdair MacIntyre's *After Virtue* (1981) works out of a similar argument. The book presents its own "epochal, historical drama" which, as much as Baudrillard's (and Kroker's), narrates a break with "the real" followed by disintegration and loss of the social. It is a rupture *after* which ethics becomes impossible other than as a simulation of what came *before*. Indeed, it is the thesis of *After Virtue* that contemporary moral judgments "are no more than *simulacra* of the moral claims of an earlier epoch, residual fragments of a teleological system of thought which has disappeared" (131). This "account of the present state of moral discourse fits with other descriptions of our cultural post-modernity," Paul Patton observes (1986, 130). For this reason, I will consider MacIntyre's work here.

After Virtue opens with "a disquieting suggestion." Imagine, MacIntyre says, that an environmental catastrophe is blamed by the public on scientists, resulting in a political movement which sets out to abolish science altogether. Laboratories are burned, scientists lynched, books and instruments destroyed. Imagine then, he says, that people some time later seek to revive science, although they have all but forgotten what it was and although all that they have to work with are fragments: "half-chapters from books, single pages from articles, not always fully legible because torn and charred" (1). What would comprise "science" in such a world would be without coherence, and would bear no relation to the tradition of science that went before. According to MacIntyre, the scenario suggests the grave disorder of contemporary ethics. What passes as ethics today "are the fragments of a conceptual scheme, parts which now lack those contexts from which their significance derived. We possess indeed simulacra of morality, we continue to use many of the key expressions. But we have—very largely, if not entirely—lost our comprehension, both theoretical and practical, of morality" (2).

The trouble, he says, began with the medieval-to-modern break from Aristotelian philosophy. Prior to this, the individual was understood as social, that is, as a member within a variety of social communities ("I am brother, cousin and grandson, member of this household, that village, this tribe" [MacIntyre 1981, 32]), and as wayfarer within a teleological whole, "placed at a certain point on a journey with set goals" such that "to move through life is to make progress—or fail to make progress—toward a given end" (32). In the medieval context, ethics comprised three elements: "untutored human nature, man-as-he-could-be-if-he-realised-his-*telos* and the moral precepts which enabled him to pass from one state to the other" (52). The notion of human *telos* was essential to this scheme, MacIntyre says, so much so that when the idea of human essence was abandoned, along with the secular rejection of theology and the scientific and philosophical rejection of Aristotelianism, the threefold framework of ethics shattered. The Enlightenment philosophers inherited the remains of this shattering, and although they attempted to mold the remnant bits and pieces into a new moral system, they failed to restore *telos* to ethics. From Kant to the present, the failure was repeated again and again, as ethics was increasingly rooted in the *individual* who, "freed from hierarchy and teleology, conceives of himself as sovereign in his moral authority" (60), but whose moral judgements are only masks for arbitrary self-will.

MacIntyre credits Nietzsche with recognizing the disorder of modern morality. "For it was Nietzsche's historic achievement to understand more clearly than any philosopher—certainly more clearly than his counterparts in Anglo-Saxon emotivism and continental existentialism—not only that what purported to be appeals to objectivity were in fact expressions of subjective will, but also the nature of the problems that this posed for moral philosophy" (107). This perceptiveness makes Nietzsche's "moral philosophy" one of the "two genuine theoretical alternatives confronting anyone trying to analyse the moral condition of our culture" (104). The other alternative is Aristotle. *After Virtue* pits these two thinkers against each other, so as to argue that Nietzsche's "moral philosophy" is false, and so as to make Nietzsche's critique of modern morality turn out in the end to be a vindication of MacIntyre's claim: that the West's repudiation of Aristotle was wrong in the first place. The choice with which *After Virtue* leaves its readers is a straightforward either/or: "*either* one must follow through the aspirations and the collapse of the different versions of the Enlightenment project until there remains only the Nietzschean diagnosis and the Nietzschean problematic *or* one must hold that the Enlightenment project was not only mistaken, but should never have been commenced in the first place. There is no third alternative" (111).

In *Whose Justice? Which Rationality?* (1988), MacIntyre continues his defence of the Aristotelian-Thomistic "tradition" over against liberal modernity, which he says detaches the person from every "tradition-informed community of discourse" and offers "no scheme of belief within which such an individual is able to find him or herself at home" (395). In *Three Rival Versions of Moral Inquiry* (1990), he again defends "tradition" against "the Nietzschean project," as well as against the "encyclopedia" of Henry Sidgwick. But with *Three Rival Versions*, MacIntyre centers his critique not on Nietzsche but on Foucault, who is held up as representative of "the post-Nietzschean enterprise" (47). I won't attempt a summary of MacIntyre's reading of Foucault, for such would require a discussion of MacIntyre's Nietzsche, a "moral philosopher" whose *position* ("the Nietzschean position") is said to be one of denial, an anti-position, and who, according to MacIntyre, "did not advance a new theory against older theories: he proposed an abandonment of theory" (49). As a "post-Nietzschean genealogist," a nihilist, Foucault "follows Nietzsche in dismissing any notion of *the* truth and correspondingly any conception of *what is* as such and timelessly as contrasted with what seems to be the case from a variety of different perspectives" (205). With the genealogical "dismissal" of the ontological position go the notions of identity, teleology, and accountability that MacIntyre takes to be essential to ethics. Foucault's discourse cannot give "any account of the identity, unity, and continuity of the self," he says. In fact, "as the phrase 'disintegration of the subject' suggests, the self which can think *différence* cannot be unitary" (208). Like Kroker, MacIntyre seems to equate heterogeneity with incoherence, and to regard ethics as incommensurable with "*différence*." For both critics, Foucault's work mirrors ethics in a state of collapse.

MacIntyre's *After Virtue* "offers the most probing and devastating analysis of the reification of moral categories under capital that we possess," Fredric Jameson exudes (1988a, 182). Indeed, Jameson's portrayal of the postmodern dissolution of coherence into "a practice of the randomly heterogeneous and fragmentary and the aleatory" (1984c, 71) sounds much like MacIntyre's description of contemporary ethics: as cut off from its surroundings as are Jameson's postmodern buildings, and no more than a reflection of the crisis of cultural, even global, fragmentation (MacIntyre 1980, 19). Jameson posits an historical rupture too: a "radical break" (1984a, vii) with tradition which he traces to the late 1950s and early 1960s, and especially to American architecture, which then becomes "the privileged terrain of struggle of postmodernism and the most strategic field in which this concept has been debated and its consequences explored" (1984b, 55). In architecture, and then beyond it to other aesthetic fields, the break with the modernist high/low, art/world dichotomy results in the introduction into the artistic realm of concepts and forms previously excluded as belonging to mass culture (see also Huyssen 1986). Postmodernism thus works itself out as "a kind of aesthetic populism" (Jameson 1984c, 54) which repudiates high modernist models of depth (concepts of the *auteur* or creative subject, and of expression, alienation and affect; distinctions between appearance and essence; the hermeneutics of deep reading, etc.) in favor of a new aesthetic "of schlock and kitsch" (55), "a new kind of flatness or depthlessness, a new kind of superficiality in the most literal sense" (60). Warhol's gilded slippers, "dead objects, banging together on the canvas like so many turnips" (60), replace Van Gogh's *Peasant Shoes*.

But given Jameson's "periodizing" approach, whereby postmodernism constitutes the "cultural logic" of what he terms, following Ernst Mandel, "third-stage capitalism," this transition is not confined to the aesthetic-architectural sphere. What has happened, he says, "is that aesthetic production today has become integrated into commodity production generally" (56), such that all of the features of "postmodernism" stand as "symbol and analogue" of our present global-cultural condition. Thus the dissolution of aesthetic depth signals no less than a universal collapse of historicity, and the absence of perspective in recent architectural spaces reflects a pervasive loss of political-social bearings, "the incapacity of our minds, at least at present, to map the great global multinational and decentered communicational network in which we find ourselves as individual subjects" (84). Jameson's "postmodernism" comprises the "dominant" or "force field" (57) out of which he reads "the impossible totality of the contemporary world system" (80).

As a cultural dominant, postmodernism subsumes the work of "the French." In a move which is similar to MacIntyre's and Kroker's, Jameson reads "French" textual practice as a reflection of late capitalist fragmentation. Like American architecture, the "French" text is an aesthetic mirror of the postmodern crisis. Thus, the eclecticism of postmodern architecture, "which randomly and without principle but with gusto cannibalizes all the architectural styles of the past and combines them in overstimulating ensembles" (66), reappears in *intertextuality*, "as the operator of a new connotation of 'pastness' and pseudo-historical depth" (67), in which the "history of models" replaces real history (67). The radically disjunctive style which cuts off a postmodern building from its surrounding city is rediscovered in *écriture*, or "schizophrenic writing" (71). The disorienting heterogeneity of architectural spaces is analogous to "*différance*" (75); and *textuality* itself is said to be a postmodern "aesthetic" (1988b, 95). For Jameson, in short, all of "[t]his new kind of discourse, generally associated with France and so-called French theory" is "to be numbered among the manifestations of postmodernism" (1983, 112).

Jameson's *The Prison House of Language* (1972) assesses the work of Lacan, Kristeva, Derrida and, through them, of the *Tel Quel* collective, as "if not ultimately revolutionary," then "at least explosively critical within the bourgeois tradition" (182). But the limitations of this work within a Marxist framework become particularly evident with Foucault, he says. For if Derrida's thought is not "wholly irreconcilable with Marxism" (183–84), Foucault so privileges "difference" as to collapse coherence altogether, reducing history "to one form of understanding among others" (194). Jameson's tone becomes more anxious and admonitory over time. In an interview published in 1987, he cites Foucault's work, "with its empty rhetoric of cutting, sorting and modifying, a kind of spatial language in which you organize data like a great bloc to be chopped up in various ways" (1987, 32), as a model of what has gone wrong.[4] Here, as in "Periodizing the 60s" (in 1988b), Jameson laments the dissolution of things, for instance, the "withering away" of philosophy, its disappearance into "theory," which "no longer draw[s] its significance from an insertion into the issues and debates of the philosophical tradition" but rather takes the form of commentary on other texts, texts "drawn from the most wildly distant disciplines (anthropology, psychiatry, literature, history of science)" and "selected in a seemingly arbitrary fashion" (1988b, 193). The "vocation" of "philosophy" is thereby displaced, he argues, for "there is no longer a tradition of philosophical problems in terms of which new positions and new statements can meaningfully be proposed," but only a discourse fashioned out of "*ad hoc*" texts, "one would want to call it disposable theory, the production of a *metabook*, to be replaced by a different one next season, rather than the ambition to express a proposition, a position, or a system with greater 'truth' value" (193). This process of dissolution reaches its apogee in the post-structuralist liberation of the signifer from "meaning proper," which generates a "new kind of textuality" in which the mind's moorings to the "real world" are definitively cut:

> The break-up of the sign in mid-air determines a fall back into a now absolutely fragmented and anarchic social reality; the broken pieces of language (the pure signifiers) now fall again into the world, as so many more pieces of material junk among all the other rusting and superannuated apparatuses and buildings that litter the commodity landscape and that strew the "collage city," the "delerious New York" of a postmodernist late capitalism in full crisis. (201)[5]

Against this dangerous dissolution into "theory" and the signifer free-floating in the void, Jameson advocates a "political" method he calls "homeopathy." The task of this new method would be to distinguish the threatening from the liberating features of postmodernism. The task is identical with the vocation Jameson ascribes to authentic "philosophy": "the discovery of truth and the repudiation of error" (194). Jameson's homeopathy has its source in the *Manifesto* where, he says, Marx "powerfully urges us to do the impossible," that is, to think capitalism "positively *and* negatively all at once" (1984c, 86). Jameson's task, derivatively, is to think third-stage capitalism "dialectically, as catastrophe and progress all together," to grasp, simultaneously, "the demonstrably baleful features" of postmodernism "along with its extraordinary and liberating dynamism" (86). The goal is to get beyond both liberalism and postmodernism to what he calls our *third possibility*: "beyond the old bourgeois ego and the schizophrenic subject of our organization society today: a *collective subject*, decentered but not schizophrenic" (1987, 45).

Jameson considers his homeopathy to be political and not ethical. For ethics is a term he associates with bourgeois individualism, the realm of individual morality and moralizing, while politics, he says, belongs to the very different realm of collective social values and practices. Moreover, ethics is no longer an option, since the moralist, "along with all the rest of us, is now so deeply immersed in postmodernist space, so deeply suffused and infected by its new cultural categories, that the luxury of the old-fashioned ideological critique, the indignant moral denunciation of the other, becomes unavailable" (1984c, 86).[6] But here is what the genealogist might diagnose as one of those "fainting spells" that are the conditions of a text's weakness as well as its strength (Foucault 1977b, 145): Jameson's homeopathic method distinguishes the "true" from the "false" according to a standard of judgment which is not itself open to judgment.[7] Homeopathy consists as much in the "comfortable stance of the taking of moral positions" (1984c, 86) as does the bourgeois moralizing that Jameson says postmodernism has rendered obsolete. His "cognitive mapping" charts a return to modernity's prescriptivist subject, and to the kind of community that demands coherence. His cognitive mapping suppresses what Derrida and Lyotard might call the heterogeneity of the addressee.

Another "fainting spell" in the body of the text: although Jameson indicts "theory" for contaminating "philosophy" with noncanonical texts, he privileges architecture as a kind of philosophy, "a way of thinking and of philosophizing, of trying to solve philosophical or cognitive problems" (1990, 143–44). Architect Frank Gehry's Santa Monica, California house has a "powerful claim on revolutionary spatiality" (126), Jameson says, for the building attempts the impossible task of "generating, so to speak, a new utopian spatial language, a new kind of sentence, a new kind of syntax, radically new words, beyond our own grammar" (147). And, although this new spatial liberation supposedly transcends the old bourgeois binaries of inside and outside, Jameson's own analysis of postmodernism seems to reinstall the borders along geopolitical and geophilosophical lines. Only a few sentences into his celebrated 1984 essay, "Postmodernism, or the Cultural Logic of Late Capitalism," the reader can see this coming. There is an immediate reference to France, and to "alarming new kinds of literary criticism, based on some new aesthetic of textuality or *écriture*" (54). Several paragraphs later, "the Foucault of the prisons book" is described as a totalizing theorist who, "by constructing an increasingly closed and terrifying machine," paralyzes "the impulses of negation and revolt" (57). But Jameson's tone changes when the discussion turns to America, and to architecture, which *is* a privileged postmodern site/sight, its spaces a delight to his eyes. To contemplate these hyperspaces, he says, is to experience a "a strange new hallucinatory exhilaration," the giddy "euphoria" of an "hysterical sublime" (76). Such is the experience of coming upon the Crocker Bank Building in downtown Los Angeles: "This great sheet of windows, with its gravity-defying two-dimensionality, momentarily transforms the solid ground on which we climb into the contents of a stereopticon, pasteboard shapes profiling themselves here and there around us" (62). And such is the delight, "the spectacle and the excitement," of Portman's Bonaventura Hotel, a postmodern hyperspace in which "it is quite impossible to get your bearings," but in which nonetheless, in the "very real pleasures" of its elevators alone, one gains the sense of a "glorious movement" (82–83).

Both the "French text" and the American building as "aesthetic" manifestations of the cultural dominant, then; but only the latter as a " 'moment of truth' within the more evident 'moments of falsehood' " of postmodernism in crisis (1984c, 86). Jameson's postmodernism dismisses "the French," and at the same time, it represents architecture as, to borrow Derrida's words, "the last fortress of metaphysics" (Derrida 1986b, 69). Only what Ihab Hassan terms "teleological" art (1974, 258) can offer Jameson the possibility of a post-postmodern social.[8] Only an imagination willing to go beyond what Richard Kearney following Jameson, calls the frivolity, the "playful parody" of deconstruction, can provide the resource for a "poetics of the possible."[9]

Giving a Send-off

The writers of concern to me in the following essays—Jacques Derrida, Jean-François Lyotard, Jacques Lacan, Julia Kristeva, Michel Foucault— display none of the "passion for periodization" from which, Jameson says, the concept of postmodernism comes (1990, 126). Indeed, their work has little to do with "postmodernism" at all. Kristeva's single essay on the topic poses itself as the question, "Postmodernism?." When the term comes up in an interview with Gérard Raulet, Foucault has to ask for help: "What are we calling post-modernity? I'm not up to date" (1988a, 33). Derrida has never ascribed to the term, is "very mistrustful whenever people identify historical breaks" and has even "set down here and there reservations with regard to this type of periodization and distribution" (1985b, 84). The future anteriority of Lacan's work calls the ordering of past-present-future into question. And even Lyotard, whose *The Post-modern Condition* has given postmodernism a certain "French" address, borrowed the term from American critics (1984, 85n1) in what, he later said, was intended as a "slightly provocative way of placing (or displacing) into the limelight the debate about knowledge" (1991b, 34), and not as an endorsement of ruptures, periodization, or the revolutionary principle that informs this view of history (25). However, through what Susan Rubin Suleiman (1991) calls a curious displacement

> whereby the French philosopher "takes the place of" all his American predecessors, a sign of what Fredric Jameson diagnosed as the absence of historical consciousness in postmodern culture—as if the memory of those who discuss postmodernism in the 1980s did not extend beyond the confines of the decade itself (111).

The Postmodern Condition, according to Suleiman, has become "the required starting point for all current discussions of postmodernism by American and English critics" (1991, 111). Perhaps this "rare instance of 'reverse importation' in the French-American theoretical marketplace" is "a sign of the snob appeal of 'genuine French imports' (or what are mistakenly thought to be such)" Suleiman suggests, but Lyotard's book emphatically "did not initiate the discourse on postmodernism" (111–12).

Why all this concern with arranging things in proper order and with posting back and forth between America and France? Suleiman's (1991) essay, "Feminism and Postmodernism: A Question of Politics," puts postmodernism back in its place: America is the site of origin. And originator of the definition: most people have now accepted "as a given," she says, that "postmodernism constitutes a totally new development or 'break' in relation to modernism" (113). Suleiman's "most people" seems to include Lyotard, whose *The Postmodern Condition*, she takes to be a "manifesto" of "poststructuralism."[10] The book is most notable for having "articulated the links between French poststructuralist philosophy and postmodern cultural practices," she says, "so that the latter could be seen—at least in the ideal sketched by Lyotard—as an instantiation of the former" (112). Thus, according to Suleiman, Lyotard positions French "poststructuralism" sequentially *before* American "postmodernism," or at least he sees the latter as an "instantiation" (a present instance, a presentable model) of the former. And Suleiman takes this concern with what comes *before* and what comes *after* to be the emphasis of *The Postmodern Condition* overall which, in keeping with "the optimism for the future that the manifesto genre requires," projects "a positive dream," the dream of a future society, "a utopian—or cautiously utopian, if such a thing is possible—version of Babel" (112).[11] A few paragraphs later, she notes that Craig Owens' 1983 article, "The Discourse of Others: Feminists and Postmodernists," uses poststructuralism and postmodernism as interchangeable terms. One *is* an instantiation of the other, she seems to conclude, since from that point on, the term poststructuralism drops out of her essay. Postmodernism takes its place.

It seems to me that the displacements of "the French" that I have been considering in this Introduction are not gestures which attempt to leave differences intact, so much as efforts to tame and to assimilate, to distinguish between *-isms* in ways that conflate one thing with another. Thus, by the time Suleiman dispatches Lyotard—at a point early in her essay—she has already assimilated *The Postmodern Condition* into her periodizing scheme. She has already claimed that Lyotard's book makes "postmodernism" and "poststructuralism" into interchangeable terms. And she has thereby reduced the "political" import of "French poststructuralism" to the practice of what she calls the "postmodern style": "appropriation, misappropriation, montage, collage, hybridization, and general mixing up of visual and verbal texts and discourses, from all periods of the past as well as from the multiple social and linguistic fields of the present" (118). This may seem to simplify the picture, and to lend plausibility to Suleiman's argument that "postmodernism" (also, if one wishes, "poststructuralism") needs "feminism" to give it political credibility, that "feminism brings to postmodernism the political guarantee postmodernism needs in order to feel respectable as an avant-garde practice" (116). But the difficulty is that "the French philosopher" who gives us what Suleiman calls a "poststructuralist manifesto" dissociates his work from historical periodization. Periodizing, for Lyotard, belongs to a thoroughly "modern" (Christian or Cartesian) chronologization (1991b, 25), to a metanarrative that equates progress with "gaining time" (1988a, xi–xvi).[12] Lyotard says that his use of the term postmodernism "has nothing to do with what is called postmodernity or postmodernism on the market of contemporary ideologies," and "nothing to do with the use of parodies or quotations of modern or modernist works as we can see it happening in architecture, painting or theatre" (1991b, 34). Lyotard's "postmodernism" has nothing to do with a present instance or presentable model, for a work can be called "postmodern," he says, only if it "allude[s] to something which does not allow itself to be made present" (1984, 84), or more precisely, if it "puts forward the unpresentable in presentation itself" (81).

Like Suleiman, Linda Hutcheon, when she argues that feminism and postmodernism "must be kept separate" (1989, 161), that "there is a major difference of orientation between the two that cannot be ignored" (142), and that this difference stems from postmodernism's lack of a so-cial-political "position,"[13] has already subsumed ("French") "poststruc-turalism" to a "postmodernism" modelled on architecture and art. Hutcheon distinguishes her "paradoxical postmodernism of complicity and critique" (11) from both from the "deliberate totalizing" (64) of Jameson and the "apocalyptic rhetoric" (1988a, 222) of Kroker. But like Jameson and Kroker, Hutcheon theorizes postmodernism as an aesthetic practice modelled on the example of postmodern architecture, architec-ture "as theorised by Paolo Portoghesi and Charles Jencks and as actual-ized by Ricardo Bofill, Aldo Rossi, Robert Stern, Charles Moore, and others" (ix). Hutcheon then argues for the "inseparability of poststruc-turalist theory and postmodern art" (Afterword 113). She claims that "the lessons learned from Derrida about textuality and deferral, or from Vattimo and Lyotard about intellectual mastery and its limits" are of a piece with the self-conscious ironies of postmodern architecture and art (1991, 112–13). And she stresses the need to go beyond postmodernism (thus, poststructuralism) to "feminism," for only the latter, she says, pro-vides an "effective theory of agency that enables a move into political *action*" (1989, 3).[14] "Complicity" may be necessary to a deconstructive critique, Hutcheon says, "though it inevitably conditions both the radicality of the kind of critique it can offer and the possibility of suggest-ing change" (1989, 152). Because feminisms want "to *change*" meaning systems (153), and not just "deconstruct" them, they should continue to resist "incorporation into the postmodern camp" (152).

A dispatching, by these critics, of "theory" back to France, but in the same gesture, its domestication within the North American institution: this is, I suggest, one political implication of beginning with postmodern-ism already defined. Another, related implication would be a stifling of the very impulses for change that these critics claim to seek. For the periodizing of postmodernism, along with the concern to position things in order and to put a project in place, represents a return to modern sub-jectivity rather than the possibility for radical change. Linearity replaces an entire system of metaphysical (hierarchical, oppositional) boundaries which, according to "the French," must be opened to change. For "the French," I might also add, serialization is in any case *impossible*. For the heterogeneous *-isms* that serializing discourses place in diachrony are always in a contaminating relationship one with the other. The contamination, a "teratological coincorporation" (Derrida, 1990, 67), spoils borders or boundaries, making quotation marks necessary around a designator such as "the French," and making the "American" scene "always more than the American scene" (80). The contamination does not erase differences, but disperses them across a (postal) network.

In the essays that follow, I will take this network to be inseparable from the text: the text, considered as an "open field" where, as Lyotard puts it in *Peregrinations*, each "phrase" arrives as something different, yet as no more "bounded" than a "cloud of thought." The text so considered suggests Foucault's peculiar sense of *catachresis*: a mode of address in which shifting boundaries contaminate things, transposing them into all kind of marvelous monsters (1986, 13–28). Monsters of the sort that Derrida refers to in "Some Statements and Truisms about Neologisms, Newisms, Postisms, Parasitisms, and Other Small Seismisms," monstrosities which "outdate and make comical all classifications or rhythms such as: after New Criticism comes an 'ism' and then a '*postism*,' and then again another 'ism,' and today still another 'ism,' etc." (1990, 79). If writing begins in the middle of such a field, with contamination always already the rule, then every definition, every delimitation of boundaries, should raise for us the (ethical) question of what difference(s) our boundaries exclude. In attentiveness to excluded differences might lie possibilities for change: this is, I think, one point of consensus among the writers whose work is the subject of the following essays. The "monsters" announce themselves "beforehand"—they are not introduced by "the French," who attempt only to respond to differences rather than to subsume them. And why not respond? Since in the responding, change might finally happen, something might "finally have a chance of happening or taking place, that's all. It isn't certain, it isn't predictable— simply, it is better that something happen. That's all: that something happen, that's what is better, that's all" (81).

That something happen (*il arrive*). Which, for Lyotard, means not that the "something" be modelled or represented, but that it be presented as what cannot be said. "In the world where 'everything is possible,' where 'nothing poses a problem,' where 'anything can be arranged,' writing that declares the impossible and exposes itself to it also remains possible," he claims (1990, 47). We could say that, for Lyotard, writing has a sort of destiny or destination to this impossible-unrepresentable, and that understood this way, the "post" of "postmodernism" signifies a procedure of "working through" to something else (1992, 80), to a something else that offers possibility for change. Kristeva also calls this something else an unthinkable or unrepresentable (1980b, 141). As a response to the unrepresentable, she says, postmodernism "writes itself with the more or less conscious intention of expanding the signifiable and thus human realm" (137). More or less. Forward and backward. Up and down. Reading is a working through the gaps: we cannot, Lacan says, overlook a certain something else that language gives us to read through its vertiginous comings and goings ("this is how I define writing") (1975, 64).

And this is how I propose to begin: by writing. By cutting loose in the midst of these ups and downs. Trying to become a reader of some unfamiliar "French" texts. The first part of this book considers two very different readings of Kant by Derrida and Lyotard. I do not attempt to "resolve" the differences between Derrida and Lyotard into a unifiable thesis. I do, however, take both of their readings to be concerned with the tone of moral philosophy and with the difficult question of the relation between uniformity of tone and imposition of social consensus. Both readings are "deconstructive," I also suggest, in the sense that both are responses to an *unrepresentable something* by which a text "deconstructs itself." The second set of essays considers the relation between psychoanalysis and the subject of ethics in the writing of Kristeva and Lacan, in their very different re-readings of Freud's unconscious as an *unrepresentable something*, an unlocalizable dis-place. Finally, I turn to Foucault's *catachresis*, a mode of writing similar to what Lyotard calls *anamnesis*: a working "down" or "through," not to an underlying "secret," but to something else, an *unrepresentable something* that might allow us to think differently than we presently think.

It isn't certain. But it might happen. That's all.

PART ONE

1

Deconstruction's Delirium

ETHICS IN ERRANT

By its very tone, the mixing of voices, genres, and codes, and the breakdown [le détraquement] of destinations, apocalyptic discourse can also dismantle the dominant contract or condordat. It is a challenge to the established admissibility of messages and to the enforcement or the maintenance of order [la police] of the destination, in short to the postal regulations [la police postale] or to the monopoly of the posts. Conversely, we could even say that every discourse or every tonal disorder, everything that untunes and becomes inadmissible in general collocution, everything that is no longer identifiable starting from established codes, from both sides of one front, will necessarily pass for or be considered mystagogic, obscurantistic, and apocalyptic. It will be made to pass for such.

Derrida, "Of an Apocalyptic Tone Recently
Adopted in Philosophy"

Jacques Derrida's "Of an Apocalyptic Tone Recently Adopted In Philosophy" was presented at the end of the 1980 Cerisy-la-Salle conference, which took as its beginning, its point of departure, his work on the end(s) of man: "*Les fins de l'homme: à partir du travail de Jacques Derrida.*"[1] In the paper, Derrida speaks "of (with) an apocalyptic tone in philosophy" (1982b, 63). He speaks of eschatological foretellings of the end of

23

this or that: of the subject, of consciousness, of history, of philosophy, of the West, of literature, of psychoanalysis, of painting, of phallogocentrism, of religion, of morals, of the earth. He speaks, then, of the corpses that the Derrida of postmodernism has been made to inherit, deconstruction having been characterized, especially in North America, as a radically apocalyptic gesture, "the absolute revelation of language as the unsayable (*as language for which there is nothing to reveal*)" (Spanos 1987, 284). It is in the name of ethics, and of no less than global survival, that philosophers have called for an end to deconstruction, its necessary death. Deconstruction, says Richard Kearney, "must be compelled to recognize *ethical* limits":

> Deconstruction too has its limits and must be made to acknowledge them . . . we must insist on the possibility, in the wake of deconstruction, of affirming some notion of a properly *human* imagination . . . we cannot shrink from such a task of reinterpretation. For to do so is to risk being submerged in a corrosive rhetoric of apocalyptic pessimism, a cultural nihilism which not only encourages feelings of paralysis and impotence but also points, in the longer term, to the possible demise of humanity itself. (1987, 42)

The wake of deconstruction ("The watch [*La veillée*] over the death or the end of philosophy, the vigil [*la veille*] by the corpse of philosophy" [1982b, 77–78]), the philosopher's fear of impotence ("there are those who adorn themselves with this new tone in philosophy, who emasculate and make a corpse of, empty [*cadavérisent*] reason" [76]): these are not just a recent (hi)story, or so Derrida suggests in his Cerisy presentation. Derrida's paper is his reading of a dated, yet contemporary, apocalyptic text, Immanuel Kant's "Of an Overlordly Tone Recently Adopted in Philosophy" (*Von einem neuerdings erhobenen vornehmen Ton in der Philosophie* (1796); French translation L. Guillermit (1975), *D'un ton grand seigneur adopté naguère en philosophie*),[2] in which Kant attacks "mystagogues" (*mystagogen*), that is, poets, pietists, mystics, visionaries, all representatives of the "old" metaphysics, whose confusion of the voice of the oracle with the voice of moral reason threatens philosophy's death.[3] Then as now, such pronouncements of the end are, for Derrida, indicative of certain ends— "symptomatic of certain political and institutional interests" (1984a, 124)—which call for deconstruction. And such deconstruction of ends seems to be Derrida's end in "Of an Apocalyptic Tone," where he concerns himself not so much with the content as with the *timbre* of an eschato-logical pitch (F *timbre*: the sonorous quality of a muscial instrument or voice; earlier, a kind of bell, a ball struck by a hammer [used in OF to render the L *tympanum*]; also in OF, a crest impressed on a legal document, whence to a postmark, a stamp). Where do they want to come to, he asks, and to what end, those who declare the imminence of the end of this or that? The question can be phrased as one of destiny (F *destin, destinée*: destiny, fate, end) or dispatch (F *envoi*: sending [thing sent]; dispatch, missive, letter; homonymous with *en voix*: in tone, in voice), of who is sending the textual *envoi* and to what destination (F *destination*: destination, intention, object, end) or what address (F *destinataire*: addressee, receiver, recipient; consignee, payee). To deconstruct a text, for Derrida, is to ask of it these questions of the *post*: "*Who is writing? To whom? And to send, to destine, to dispatch what? To what address?*" (1987b, 5).[4]

On the one hand, I will suggest in what follows that Derrida's decon-structive reading of "Of an Overlordly Tone" attempts the unveiling (G *apokalupsis*: uncovering, disclosure) of a series of conceptual oppositions through which Kant positions a rational, masculine person-subject as both the sender and receiver of ethics, thus as the limit (closure) of the philosophical text. In this first gesture, *apokalupto* is especially "to un-cover the ear" of Kant's moral philosophy, "the distinct, differentiated, articulated organ that produces the effect of proximity, of absolute prop-erness" ("Tympan" in 1982a, xvii), and that establishes moral philosophy as phonocentric. Derrida's reading does not end there, however, as an ac-complished unmasking or dismantling ("destruction") of this philoso-phy's binary hierarchical scheme, for *on the other hand*, deconstruction's apocalypse also reveals that Kant's text is folded inside-out "I would say like a glove" (1982b, 76). In a second gesture, simultaneous with the first, Derrida's reading re-marks this site of the fold, opening "Of an Overlordly Tone" to its difference from itself, finding inside the essay the very elements of mystagogy that Kant banishes to the outside of his text. This interfolded structure confounds what we might have thought were the (internal and external) boundaries of Kant's essay, and it lays bare the scene of writing that rational philosophy so resolutely conceals. The self-identity of addressor and addressee is no longer certain, for through this second gesture of deconstruction, Kant's text becomes apocalyptic (*apocalypse*: spurious and enigmatic literature, revealing mysteries of vi-sions and dreams; composite; sensuous; pseudonymous). Deconstruc-tion's responsibility, Derrida suggests, is to this apocalyptic autograph.

Apocalypse

Kant's "Of an Overlordly Tone Recently Adopted in Philosophy" is a twenty-page lampoon which indicts mystagogues for changing or rupturing philosophy's uniform pitch. Mystagogues proffer supernatural or intuitive knowledge as a supplement or surrogate of rational faith, Kant claims, and this failure to distinguish between the voice of moral reason and the voice of the oracle occasions what he terms a *Verstimmung* (G *Verstimmung*: discord, disorder, upset; *Verstimmen*: to put out of tune), an untuning of philosophy. Derrida suggests that an implicit homogeneous/ heterogeneous binary informs this condemnation of mystagogues who pose as philosophers. "Isn't the dream or the ideal of philosophic discourse, of philosophical address [*allocution*], and of the writing supposed to represent that address, isn't it to make the tonal difference inaudible— and with it a whole desire, affect, or scene that works (over) the concept as contraband?," Derrida asks. "Through what is called neutrality of tone, philosophical discourse must also guarantee the neutrality or at least the imperturbable serenity that should accompany the relation to the true and the universal" (1982b, 66). For Kant, the mystagogic tone marks a deviation from the norm of philosophical address, Derrida says: "the tonal difference does not pass for the essentially philosophic" (67).

But Kant is not concerned in his essay with the pure phenomenon of tonality, Derrida suggests, so much as with a manner or mannerism of taking on airs, "the grand air of those pretentious people who elevate their voice" (70) or who "place themselves out of the common" (69), the presumption of the mystagogic impostors. Kant does not "indict the pitch or loftiness of the overlordly tone when it is just, natural, or legitimate" (70), then, but only "takes aim at raising the tone when an upstart [*parvenu*] authorizes himself in this by giving himself airs and by erecting usurped signs of social membership" (70). His homogeneous/heterogeneous binary functions as a high/low dichotomy, and as with every such dichotomy, "we are not dealing with the peaceful coexistence of a *vis-à-vis*, but rather with a violent hierarchy. One of the two terms governs the other (axiologically, logically, etc.), or has the upper hand" (1981b, 41). The mystagogues must be excluded from philosophy's site.

Derrida's reading of Kant's "Of an Overlordly Tone" uncovers a whole series of binary oppositional pairs that work this way to privilege philosophy as an order of homogeneity and meaning and to banish "mystagogy" to philosophy's outside. Central among these binaries is the hierarchy philosophy/poetry: "Kant does not doubt this: the new preachers need to pervert philosophy into poetry in order to give themselves grand airs, to occupy through simulacrum and mimicry the place of the great, to usurp thus a power of symbolic essence" (1982b, 77). For Kant, says Derrida, the mystagogues "replace the evidences and proofs with " 'analogies,' " " 'versimilitudes' " (" *'Analogien, Wahrscheinlichkeiten'* "). . . . These are their words. Kant cites them and calls us to witness: you see, they are not true philosophers; they resort to poetic schemas" (75). It is the contamination of philosophical reason that Kant so vociferously resists, railing against the use of the figure "emasculation of reason" in Schlosser's 1795 translation into German of the *Letters* of Plato, ruling the figure inadmissible because, as Derrida says, "it takes the place of proof" (76), and insisting throughout "Of an Overlordly Tone" on the absolute distinction "between metaphor and concept, literary mystagogy and true philosophy" (76).

What is put at risk by the mystagogue's confusion of *logos* and *mythos* is the boundary between intelligibility and sense. Here Derrida points to "the extreme subtlety" of Kant's objection to the mystagogues: "they believe they know what is solely thinkable and reach through feeling alone the universal laws of practical reason" (72). Kant knows, however, that the voice of practical reason has nothing to do with vision or touch, that, as Derrida writes:

> it describes nothing; it says nothing of the describable [*de descriptible*]; it dictates, prescribes, orders. Kant also names it in Latin: *dictamen rationis*. . . . [I]t resounds in every man, for every man has in him the idea of duty . . . orders him to sacrifice his drives, to resist seductions, to forego his desires. And the voice promises me nothing in return; it assures me of no compensation. It is sublime in this; it orders, mandates, demands, commands without giving anything in exchange. . . . That is the *true* mystery—Kant also calls it *Geheimnis* . . . but it is no longer the false mystery of the mystagogues. It is the mystery at once domestic, intimate, and transcendent, the *Geheimnis* of practical reason, the sublimity of moral law and moral voice. The mystagogues fail to recognize that *Geheimnis*; they confuse it with a mystery of vision and contact, whereas moral law never gives itself to be seen or touched. (72–73)

Derrida writes in *Of Grammatology* (12) that logocentrism assumes an "absolute proximity of voice and being, of voice and the meaning of being, of voice and the ideality of meaning." And in Kant's account of the moral law as a voice that resounds in every man, that "strikes in him in a rather percussive and repercussive way" (1982b, 72), and that is "more auditory, more audible than the mystagogic oracle still contaminated with feeling, illumination, or intuitive vision, contact and mystical tact ('ein . . . mystischer Takt,' Kant says)" (73), Derrida finds this same essential link to the *phone*. For Kant, Derrida says, the *Geheimnis* of moral reason is "more in tune with the essence of the voice that hears/understands itself but neither touches nor sees itself" (73) than is the false mystery of the mystagogues, and "in its very transcendence the moral voice is nearer, and thus more auto-affective, more autonomous" (73) than is the mystagogic oracle.[5] Kant's moral law passes through the voice: gives itself to be heard from within, then speaks through the mouth of the moral philosopher. Mouth to ear, the moral law derives from and is thought to depend on "full presence or full speech," to use Derrida's words from "Economimesis" (18). In that essay, he suggests that Kant's *Anthropology* privileges hearing among the five senses, and that the third *Critique* discovers in hearing a sort of *universal tongue*: "Between the concept and the system of hearing-oneself-speak, between the intelligible and speech, the link is privileged. One must use the term hearing-oneself-speak [*le s'entendre-parler*] because this structure is auto-affective; in it the mouth and the ear cannot be dissociated" (19).

The mystagogues, then, might be likened to the deaf of Kant's *Anthropology*, for they lack access to the logos itself, and like the deaf who resort to lip reading or mechanical prosthesis, they cannot dissociate intelligibility from sense.[6] Hence, the delirium that results from the mystagogue's overlordly tone. Derrida points out that "*Verstimmen*, which Guillermit translates not without reason by *délirer*, to be delirious, is first of all to put out of tune [*désaccorder*], when we speak of a stringed instrument [*instrument à cordes*], or yet, for example, a voice. This is currently said of a piano. Less strictly this signifies to derange, to put out of order, to jumble" (1982b, 72). And the *Verstimmung* of which Kant speaks, he says, is indeed a matter of *disorder*—of philosophy's history, filiation, origin. For the instant the mystagogues come on the scene, "the name philosophy loses its signification or its original reference" (68), an event which Kant seems to locate near the beginning of philosophy, if not in the figure of its first father. Kant is given a "devilish job" with Plato, Derrida observes, for although his authentic writings make him the father of rational philosophy, his *Letters*, just translated into German by Schlosser, make him the father of delirium, and Kant thus faces the difficulty of "distinguishing between the good Plato and the bad Plato, the true and the false, his authentic writings and his more or less reliable or apocryphal ones" (73). Kant must divide Plato so that mystagogy does not usurp philosophy's original grounding in rational evidences and proofs.

Not only the rational foundation of philosophy, however, but also its fundamental principle of social equality is at issue for Kant in this division of the good Plato from the bad Plato. What is intolerable to Kant in the letter-writer Plato, Derrida suggests, "is aristocratic esotericism— Kant cites that Letter recommending not divulging secrets to the crowd—a cryptophilness added to a mystical interpretation of mathematics. . . . And this mathematizing mysticism, this idolatry of figures and numbers always goes hand in hand with phenomena of sect, cryptopolitics, indeed superstitious theophany that Kant opposes to rational theology" (74). As with the bad Plato, so with the mystagogues, their esoteric visions and their penchant for private cults. Derrida: "The mystagogues claim to possess as it were in private the privilege of a mysterious secret. . . . They never transmit the secret to others in the current language, only by initiation or inspiration. The mystagogue is *philosophus per initiationem* or *per inspirationem*" (69). Mystagogy implies secrecy, and so threatens philosophy's coveted principle of the equality of rational selves: "The tone leaps and is raised higher when the voice of the oracle takes you aside, speaks to you in a private code, and whispers secrets to you in uncovering your ear for you, jumbling, covering, or parasitizing the voice of reason that speaks equally in each and maintains the same language for all" (72).

For all of these reasons among others, Kant must separate philosophy from mystagogy. "Philosophy has always insisted upon this: thinking its other. Its other: that which limits it, and from which it derives its essence, its definition, its production" (Derrida 1982a, x). And if, as Derrida says, the vehicle by which this separation has always been effected is the contract or concordat which philosophy offers to its outside ("if it has constituted itself according to this purposive *entente* with its outside, if it has always intended to hear itself speak, in the same language, of itself and of something else" [xii]), we should not be surprised that Kant's "Of an Overlordly Tone" concludes by proposing a contract or condordat with the mystagogues. For Derrida, the terms of this contract are utterly important, more important "than the whole combinative strategy" (1982b, 78) between the two parties. What, according to Kant's contract, "can deeply bind the two adversary parties and procure for them a neutral ground of reconciliation for yet speaking together about the suitable tone?" (78), he asks. What does the contract propose that the two parties exclude as philosophy's inadmissible *other*? "What is the *inadmissible*?" (78) becomes, for Derrida, the fundamental question to ask of Kant. What is the *inadmissible* of modern moral philosophy? The proposed social contract is the one part of Kant's "Of an Overlordly Tone" which Derrida quotes at length:

> But what is the good of all this conflict between two parties that at bottom share the same good intention: to make men wise and honest? It is noise about nothing, a discord founded on a misunderstanding, which calls less for reconciliation than for reciprocal explanation in order to conclude an accord, an accord that makes a still more profound harmony for the future.
>
> The veiled goddess before which we on both sides bend our knees is the moral law in us in its invulnerable majesty. We certainly perceive its voice, and we understand very clearly its commandments. But in hearing it we doubt whether it comes from man and whether it originates from the all-powerfulness of his very own reason, or whether it emanates from some other being, whose nature is unknown to man and who speaks to him through his own proper reason. At bottom we would perhaps do better to exempt ourselves entirely from this research, for it is simply speculative, and what (objectively) devolves upon us to do remains the same, let one found it on one or the other principle. The only difference is that the didactic procedure of leading the moral law in us back to distinct concepts according to a logical method is alone properly *philosophical*, whereas the procedure consisting in personifying this law and in making of the reason that morally commands a veiled Isis (even when we attribute no other properties to it than those the first method discovers in it) is an *esthetic* manner of representing (*eine ästhetische Vorstellungsart*) exactly the same object. It is indeed permitted to rely on this manner, since one has already started by leading the principles back to their pure state, in order to give life to this idea thanks to a sensible, though only analogical, presentation (*Darstellung*), but not without always running some risk of falling into an exalted vision, which is the death of all philosophy. (79–80)

Kant asks the mystagogues "to get rid of the veiled goddess before which they both tend to kneel . . . no longer to personify the moral law or the voice that incarnates it," Derrida writes, "above all not under the 'esthetic,' sensible, and beautiful form of this veiled Isis" (79). Such exclusion "will be the condition for understanding/hearing the moral law itself, the unconditioned, and for understanding/hearing ourselves. In other words, and this is a trenchant motif for thought of the law and the ethical today, Kant calls for placing the law above and beyond, not the person, but personification and the body" (79), the body of (as) woman. Isis* is the *inadmissible* of Kant's moral philosophy, according to a social contract which places the law above the body (*mind/body*), and which represents materiality, the body, as woman (*man/woman*).

Female sexuality, femininity: The name Isis, Greek form of the Egyptian hieroglyph "throne," signifies motherhood, creation of the King. Isis, celebrated goddess of Egypt, Greece, and Rome, gives birth, perhaps once as an independent Mother Goddess (Kant, in the *Critique of Judgement* [179], refers to her as "Mother *Nature*"). From antiquity, she is called by many names—Astarte, Hera, Selene, Demeter, Aphrodite—suggesting her universal motherhood (Derrida 1982b, 79: "the universal principle of feminity"). Isis, the prototype of woman.

The veil of feminine secrecy: Isis, called "the Mother in Magic," gives birth to mystagogy. In the Graeco-Roman world, her cult takes the form of a mystery religion presided over by priests and involving initiatory rites, festive banquets, the interpretation of dreams, and other cultic rituals which are kept to the rule of secrecy (Kant [1790] 1978, 179: "veil before her face").

Emasculation of the logos: Not all versions of the Isis-Osiris myth portray her as the slayer-castrater of her husband (Derrida 1982b, 79: "murderess of Osiris all of whose pieces she later recovers, except for the phallus"). In Plutarch's account, for instance, Set (Seth) assassinates, then dismembers, his brother Osiris, but even here, there is an emasculation of sorts, since in the absence of Osiris, Isis conceives and gives birth to Horus. Barbara Walker (455), following S. G. F. Brandon and E. O. James, summarizes the Isis-Osiris legend as follows:

> Isis swallowed Osiris the savior and brought him back to life. He was reincarnated as the child Horus, or else as the ithyphallic moon-god, Min, or Menu, "He who impregnates his mother." He was annually torn to pieces and reassembled except for his lost penis. Isis made him a new penis of clay, then gave it—and him—new life by invoking her own holy names as life-giver and death-giver: "Behold, I have found thee lying there. Weary is the great one . . . O Osiris, live, stand up thou unfortunate one that liest there! I am Isis. I am Nephthys."

For Kant, then, *Verstimmung* signifies not only the displacement of philosophy's (rational, paternal) origin but also, as Derrida puts it, "the derailment . . . the disorder or the delirium of the destination (*Bestimmung*)" (84), and in calling for the exclusion of Isis, Kant is thus attempting to insure philosophy's proper addressee or end, "the unity of destination, the self-identity of some addressee [*destinataire*] or sender [*destinateur*]" (84). "The tone's pitch is tied to tension," Derrida suggests: "it has a bond to the bond, to the bond's more or less tight tension" (69). The word tone (G *tōnos*, L *tonus*, F *ton*) "first signified the tight ligament [*le ligament tendu*], the cord, rope when it is woven or braided, the cable, the strap," he reminds us, and as such it is "the privileged figure of everything that is subject to stricture" (69), of every taut reference that bonds sender to receiver, sign to thing. "*Tonion* is the ligament as band and surgical bandage" (69), he adds, suggesting that the apocalyptic tone which bands (F *bander*: to stretch, to bond, to enshroud; also, to get an erection) the corpse of this or that might always proceed from the same (father's) place of emission, might always be postmarked to the same address (F *ton*: tone; also the second person singular masculine possessive adjective). Kant's apocalyptic tone wants "to come or arrive at itself," Derrida concludes, "to seduce in order to lead to itself" (84), to lead back to the person, the philosophical author, as patriarchal subject-origin of moral truth, a subject who constitutes himself, and his philosophy, by means of a separation from, and suppression of, his other as object-outside (*subject/object, self/other, person/nonperson*).

Autography

From a man who offers personal details only grudgingly ("Ah, you want me to tell you things like 'I-was-born-in-El-Biar-in-the-suburbs-of-Algiers-in-a-petit-bourgeois-Jewish-family-which-was-assimilated-but . . ." [1988a, 74]), this statement: "everything that I write, one quickly sees, is terribly autobiographical" (Finas et al. 1973, 309). Why *terribly* (F *terrible*: dreadful, frightening, awful, catastrophic; exceedingly, excessively, very greatly)? Claude Lévesque asks Derrida this question in the "Roundtable on Autobiography" published in *The Ear of the Other*, suggesting that the adverb in this case signifies excess and extreme, implies that "one has overstepped the mark (of discourse and of knowledge) . . . that there has been a crossing at the limit" (Derrida 1985b, 72). Derrida's reply to Lévesque refers to "one of the scenes of the *double bind* in *Glas*," the scene of the signature, "where one loses what one wins and wins what one loses" (77). One of those terribly autobiographical texts, *Glas* disarticulates Derrida's proper name: "By a stroke of his autobiographical D, he would change semination into dis-semination, sowing into scattering. . . . The debris of d-words is scattered all over the pages" (Spivak 1977, 23–24). At work in this play with his name, says Derrida, is the desire to lose it, a desire which cannot be fulfilled, for "[b]y disseminating or losing my own name, I make it more and more intrusive; I occupy the whole site, and as a result my name gains more ground. The more I lose, the more I gain by conceiving my proper name as the common noun, '*derrière le rideau*,' and so on" (1985b, 76–77). The more Derrida inserts his name into the body of the text, the more he *erects* it into a monument, a phallic colossus, but in this process he also loses the identity or ownership of his name, lets it become a part of the text, so that "[t]he erection-tomb falls" (1984c, 56). "The *seing* falls (to the tomb[stone])" (1986a, 2).

As Derrida emphasizes in "Signature Event Context," this *double bind* or *double band* of the signature belongs to the very structure of the proper name, indeed to the structure of every sign which, though it may be intended to re-present, to make present, always entails absence and lack. For instance, "[a] written sign is proffered in the absence of the receiver," he says, meaning not only that "at the moment when I am writing, the receiver may be absent from my field of present perception" but more importantly that "[i]n order for my 'written communication' to retain its function as writing, i.e., its readability, it must remain readable despite the absolute disappearance of any receiver, determined in general" (1988c, 7). Moreover, "[w]hat holds for the receiver holds, also, for the same reasons, for the sender or the producer" (8), whose future absence or death will not, in principle, hinder the readability of the writing, any more than will the loss of the immediate context of the sign's production, "what its alleged author-scriptor consciously intended to say at the moment he wrote it" (9). For writing to be writing, in other words, it must be *apocalyptic*: it cannot be tied to the presence of an identifiable subject who in a given context produced it ("it leaps [*saute*] from one place of emission to the other" (1982b, 87), and it cannot be predestined to such and such a person ("it goes from one destination, one name, and one tone to the other" [87]). The apocalypse, for Derrida, is "the structure of every scene of writing" (87), though this scene may be "dissembled under the desire for light, well hidden (*eukalyptus*, as is said of the tree whose calycine limb remains closed after flowering), well hidden under the avowed desire for revelation" (83). Gayatri Spivak notes:

When a man writes, he is in a structure that needs his absence as its necessary condition (writing is defined as that which can necessarily be read in the writer's absence), and entails his pluralization. . . . Writers resist this troubling necessity and desire to record the living act of a sole self—an auto-bio-graphy. Whatever the argument of a document, the marks and staging of this resistance are its "scene of writing." When a person reads, the scene of writing is usually ignored and the argument is taken as the product of a self with a proper name. Writers and readers are thus accomplices in the ignoring of this scene of writing. The accounts given of texts are informed by this complicity. (Spivak 1984, 19–20)

Derrida's terribly autobiographical texts foreground the apocalypse of writing as drama, or so he indicates in his Cerisy presentation when he says of *Glas*, for instance, that its "columns are constantly shaken by apocalyptic agitations and laughs on the subject of the apocalypse" and that in a certain moment it "mixes the remains of genres and of John, the one of the Gospel, of the Apocalypse, and of Genet" (1982b, 90); and when he refers similarly to *La Carte postale*, "where the allusions increase to the Apocalypse and to its arithmosophy, where everything speculates on the figures and notably seven, the 'written seven,' the angels, 'my angel,' the messengers and the postmen [*facteurs*], prediction, the announcement of the news, the holocaustic 'burning,' and all phenomena of *Verstimmung*, of the changing of tone, of the mixing of genres, of *destinerrance*, if I can say that, or of *clandestination*, so many signs of more or less bastard apocalyptic filiation" (91). Exhibited in these texts is the double bind (*da: fort*) not only of Derrida's signature (like a post card, "neither legible nor illegible, open and radically unintelligible" [1987b, 79]), but also of the signatures of Freud, Lacan, Hegel, Jean Genet, and John of Patmos, signer of the biblical Apocalypse.[7] What Derrida (1988c, 7) terms the "logic of iterability" (*iter*, f. Sk *itara*: other) bears on every autograph. And it is the point of his "second gesture" of deconstruction to lay bare this iterability in Kant's "Of an Overlordly Tone."

Among other things, then, Derrida's reading of the essay exposes "a spectrography of the tone and of the changing of tone" (1982b, 93) which marks a gap in relation to the philosophic norm which Kant erects. That the essay is a lampoon, for instance, suggests in itself a deviation from philosophy's atonal norm. Even as he faults the mystagogues for departing from philosophy's uniform tone, Kant lampoons his adversaries, his comments "marked with the tone he gives himself . . . with his satiric or polemical verve" (67). Kant "overwhelms with his sarcasm" (67) the mystagogue's mixing and changing of tone, deviating himself from the tonal neutrality, the uniformity and objectivity, that he claims for philosophic address. "Naturally, even when he fights like this, Kant declares that he does not like warfare" Derrida writes (78); even as he "takes aim" (70) at the changing of tone; even as he "fires off his dart" and "multiplies his sarcastic remarks" (75). By his very tone, Kant places himself on both sides of the battle at once, shows that he cannot maintain the philosophical opposition same/different. Wandering over the border philosophy/ mystagogy, his tone "constrains the signature desire" (Derrida 1986c, 20), the desire or drive for the mastery of philosophy. ("To deconstruct a text is to disclose how it functions as desire, as a search for presence and fulfilment which is interminably deferred" [1984a, 126].)

Neither can Kant maintain the separation he imposes between concept and poetico-metaphorical trope. Derrida plays with numerous instances in Kant's essay where myth parasitizes philosophy, and where metaphor displaces the bond between the name philosophy and its rational referent. For instance, the bond between philosophy and clarity (revelation, the sun) is at issue, Derrida suggests, in Kant's chiding of the mystagogues for saying that we can have only a presentiment, a trace, of the sun, for giving us "only a theatrical sun (*Theatersonne*)," only "a chandelier in sum [*un lustre en somme*]" (1982b, 75). And if the mystagogic *Theatersonne* stands between philosophy and its revelation, so does the veil of Isis, which they would make thin but not raise. "[T]hin to what point" is Kant's question; Derrida observes, "[p]robably not thin enough" (75). Kant does not escape the sun, the veil, nor even the figure "emasculation of reason," Derrida points out. Kant's indictment of the figure exemplifes what it rejects:

> And Kant immediately turns the argument inside out, I would say like a glove: "whereas, nevertheless," he says, "precisely in these *a priori* principles does practical reason find an exact sentiment that it never otherwise had a presentiment of, and indeed rather by the empirical that is falsely attributed to it (this very fact is what makes it improper for a universal legislation) is it emasculated and paralyzed (*entmannt und gelähmt*)." (76)

Derrida's reading foregrounds the alterity of this scene, where images of the veil of Isis, of castration, of the raising of the veil ("To raise the veil of Isis here is *aufheben* ("'*da er den Schleier der Isis nicht aufheben kann*'")" (75)), of the sun, and of apocalyptic unveiling, are carried along "in the same tropic movement" (1982a, 218). An apocalyptic movement, which occasions for Derrida a revelation of sorts: that Kant's essay marks the catastrophe (G *katastrophe*: an overturning, a sudden turn; a violent change in the order of things; G *tropos*: turn, turning, figure of speech; in Gregorian music, a short cadence at the close of a melody; *tropology*: speaking by tropes; also, a moral discourse, an interpretation of scripture relating to morals; G *strophe*: a repetition; a counter-turn; a musical metre) of philosophy's "familiar" tone. For "[t]he mystagogues make a scene, that is what interests Kant," says Derrida. "But at what moment do the mystagogues come on stage and at times go into a trance? At what moment do they begin to create the mysterious?" (68). Kant is unable to locate for philosophy a simple origin uncorrupted by materiality and myth. "The *double bind* again of filiation" (73): Kant finds only a Plato who is different from himself; the father of philosophy as both mystagogue and *Aufklärer*; the ancient interdependence of literature and philosophy.[8]

The double bind of filiation. The impossibility of origin, of an original plenitude or proximity between *logos* and voice, is the undoing of Kant's phonocentrism, of the hierarchy he establishes between speech and writing, between intelligibility and sense. "Why did I feel inclined, at this moment of my reading of an overlordly tone, to add this document to the dossier (if I can say that) of *La Carte postale*?," Derrida asks.* "Or

---

*An autobiographical incident recorded in *The Post Card*: Derrida is in the Bodleian library in Oxford with Jonathan and Cynthia Culler, who lead him to a table where, laid out under glass among hundreds of displayed reproductions, is a post card bearing a duplication of the Matthew Paris painting of Socrates and Plato. Socrates, seated at a desk, appears to be writing; Plato stands behind him. Derrida refers to the post card as "my small library apocalypse" (11). Viewing it, he says, occasions a "revelatory catastrophe" (12). For if, as we have all believed, Socrates did not write, came before Plato who wrote more or less at his diction, then there is between this couple "an order of generations, an irreversible sequence of inheritance" (20). Speech before writing, and with that the entire order of western metaphysics: "Now, my post card, this morning when I am raving about it or delivering it [*quand je la délire ou la délivre*] in the state of jealousy that has always terrified me, my post card naively overturns everything. In any event, it allegorizes the catastrophic unknown of the order. Finally one begins no longer to understand what to come [*venir*], to come before, to come after, to foresee [*prévenir*], to come back [*revenir*] all mean" (21).

yet to arrange it in what is called *dossier* therein, between the word and the thing, the word *dossier* packed with all the backs [*dos*] with which the note and the syllable punctuate the 'Envois' on each page, at Socrates's back and on the back of the postcard, with all the words in *do* and with the back [*dossier*] of the chair, of the partition between Socrates and Plato?" (73). *Kant is writing.* He writes his account of the moral law as a voice uncontaminated by sense, and thus must avail himself of the same sort of mechanical prosthesis that relegates both the deaf and the mystagogues to an otherness outside of philosophy. A necessary connection exists between ethics (voice, reason) and writing ("The one in the other, the one in front of the other, the one after the other, the one behind the other" [1987b, 19]), and as with Plato so with Kant, writing betrays an "essential drift" (1988c, 8).

And as with Kant, so with Derrida, the essential alterity of writing is a matter of the veil. Over against mystagogy's emasculation of the *logos* and its veiling of reason, Kant calls for "philosophy's finally open and unveiled future" (1982b, 78). But his drive for the mastery of philosophy goes unfulfilled, at least in Derrida's reading (translation, citation, iteration) of "Of an Overlordly Tone" which, by listening for tonal deviations, transforms and regenerates the text. The virginal intactness of Kant's *logos/mythos*, intelligible/sensible, male/female, inside/outside boundaries is not preserved, as the father of philosophy gives birth to mystagogy, to an "aleatory errance" (95) which marks the catastrophe of his apocalyptic unveiling. Deconstruction folds mystagogy into philosophy, and so reinscribes the philosopher's autograph as a graphic of the hymen or veil (*hymen* F > G > L > *suere*, to seam, sew > Sk *syuman*, ligature, band: membranous fold; goddess of marriage [Demeter-Isis]; veil of the goddess's temple; Calliope: "she of the beautiful voice").

Apostrophe

Why should "ethicists" concern themselves with deconstruction "given the urgency of 'the rest of the world' " (Spivak 1884, 20)?[9] For by the Enlightenment standards of today's dominant moral philosophy, deconstruction is mystagogy, a postmodern *Verstimmung* which displays in its corpus all the traits of the non-philosophical. That deconstruction inscribes *différance* does not, for one thing, "appear to be a very good tone in philosophy and so marks already a gap in relation to the norm of philosophical discourse" (1982b, 66). Deconstruction also deviates from the norm of uniformity in that it addresses the non-philosophical, perverts philosophy into poetry, intermixes literary and philosophical texts.[10] But its moral failure ("irresponsibility") is said to be more serious yet, for those who denounce deconstruction "suspect those they call 'deconstructionists' of forming a sect, a brotherhood, an esoteric corporation, or more vulgarly, a clique, a gang, or (I quote) a 'mafia' " (1989a, 18). What is deemed intolerable in Derrida, the sender of post cards, is the same estericism that Kant detects in the letter-writer Plato, the same cryptopolitics that collapses rationality "into unintelligibility, pseudo-questions, pseudo-arguments, and *mystery-mongering*" and that "turns philosophy into a cult of personality with the 'new' French philosophers as the priest class exclusively entitled to interpret the obscure and oracular utterances" (Howey 1985, 91, italics mine).[11] Then as now: "*Mystagogein* is indeed this: to lead, initiate into the mystery; that is the mystagogue's or the initiatory priest's function. This *agogic* function of the leader of men, *il Duce*, the *Führer*, the *leader* places him above the crowd he manipulates through the intermediary of a small number of initiates gathered into a sect with a 'crypted' language, a band, a clique or a small party with its ritualized practices" (1982b, 69).[12]

Derrida's deconstructive reading of Kant's "Of aAn Overlordly Tone" suggests that this either/or dichotomy philosophy/mystagogy belongs to an entire hierarchical, oppositional apparatus which sends out a text as destined to return to its self. As the apocalyptic unveiling of this apocalyptic apparatus, deconstruction may mark a "critical moment" akin to the "Kantian caesura in the time [*temps*, beat, tempo] of philosophy" (1982b, 66). Deconstruction may signal a crisis concerning "the very concept of crisis or of critique" (1992c, 6). *On the one hand*, then, we might ask, as Emmanuel Levinas does, whether Derrida's work cuts "into the development of Western thinking with a line of demarcation similar to that of Kantianism, which separated dogmatic philosophy from critical philosophy" (Levinas 1991, 3). We might ask whether deconstruction indicates that we are "again at the end of a naïveté, of an unsuspected dogmatism which slumbered at the base of that which we took for critical spirit" (3). But deconstruction's end is not the end of ethics or moral philosophy, for *on the other hand*, and as distinct "from a simple progressive demystification in the style of the *Lumières*" (1982b, 90), deconstruction comes on the scene as "an apocalypse without apocalypse, an apocalypse without vision, without truth, without revelation" (94). Its dispatches, *as apocalyptic*, are "without message and without destination, without sender or decidable addressee, without last judgment, without any other eschatology than the tone of the 'Come' " (94).

This "Come" is an apostrophe that resounds through several of Derrida's texts.[13] In "Of an Apocalyptic Tone," the apostrophe cites back to the "Come" which echoes in the Johannine Apocalypse each time the Lamb opens one of the seven seals, again in Chapters 17 and 21, and in a chorus of final repetitions which occur at "the end of ends" (1982b, 92), at the moment of the (double bind of the) signature, when John receives from the angelic messenger the order not to seal his text. The Johannine "Come" does not come from John. For although John is the writer, he is not the author of the biblical Apocalypse. When John speaks, Derrida points out, he speaks by citing another, he speaks by citing Jesus. Or rather, when John writes, he "appears to transcribe what he says by recounting that he cites Jesus the moment Jesus dictates to him to write" (85). John does not write as a determinable sender, that is, but rather as one who responds: " 'write, *grapson*.' . . . Write and send, dictates the voice come from behind, in the back of John" (85–86). And even before this narrative *scene*, there occurs in the Apocalypse what Derrida calls "a kind of title or name tag [*médaille*] come from one knows not where" (86) which indicates that John receives his dictation through the medium of an angelic messenger, thus that the apocalyptic dispatch is bound to yet another voice. With each repetition of "Come," the dispatches and messengers increase so that, as Derrida puts it, there is "an interlacing of voices" in the dictated or addressed writing: "so many sendings, *envois*, so many voices, and this puts so many people on the telephone line" (86–87).

The text called the Apocalypse is also apocalyptic.[14] Derrida takes the Johannine apostrophe, he says, as "an explicit reference" (90) of the apocalyptic structure of language, "that is, of the divisible dispatch [*envoi*] for which there is no self-presentation nor assured destination" (87). For in his reading, the biblical "Come" comes from an other, "as if it [*ça*] began by responding" (92), and so is not an authorial summons. It "does not address itself" (94):

> Come from the other already as a response and a citation without past present, "Come" supports no metalinguistic citation. . . . "Come" no more lets itself be stopped and examined [*arraisonner*] by an onto-theo-eschatology than by a logic of the event. . . . "Come" marks in itself, in oneself, neither a desire nor an order, neither a prayer nor a request [*demande*]. . . . That

"Come," I do not know what *it is.* . . . "Come" cannot come
from a voice or at least not from a tone signifying "I" or "self," a
so-and-so (male or female) in my "determination." . . . It is a
drift [*une dérive*] underivable from the identity of a determination. "Come" is *only* derivable, absolutely derivable, but only
from the other. . . . "*Come*" is apocalyptic. (93–94)

As similarly derivable, "*only* derivable, absolutely derivable," the
"Come" which breaks into Derrida's writing does not come from Derrida.
"Come," he says in his Cerisy paper, we cannot not deconstruct. "In light
of today," we might say in the interests of survival, "[w]e cannot and we
must not—this is a law and a destiny—forgo the *Aufklärung*" (1982b,
82). Each time philosophy takes on an apocalyptic tone, we cannot not
ask ourselves: *Who is writing? To whom? And to send, to destine, to dispatch
what? To what address?* This is a call to deconstruction, but it is not
Derrida's call. The apocalyptic structure of language summons with the
apostrophe, "Come." It is what Derrida refers to elsewhere (1992a) as the
"deconstructible structure" itself to which deconstruction responds.
While it can be said then, that *read deconstructively*, Kant's essay is not
either philosophy or mystagogy but "a *différantielle* contamination between the two" (1992a, 38), a deconstructive reading does not give
Kant's text this *différantielle* or deconstructible structure. Derrida does not
move something from the outside to the inside of Kant's essay. The
mystagogy which Kant casts outside is inside his text, which spoils the
inside/outside dichotomy. The other to which deconstruction responds is
already there in the same.[15]

Derrida suggests that we have a duty to respond to the "Come"
which precedes and calls every reader and writer. We are answerable to
an other that leaves its trace in a text. This means that we have a duty
not to partake in the apocalypticism of today's *postal police* which, in the
interests of "ruses, traps, trickeries, seductions, the engines of war and of
pleasure, all the interests of the apocalyptic tone today" (1982b, 87), re-
duces or gears down the text's voices and tones so as to ensure its return
to an authorial self. Above all, we have a duty not to reduce *responsibility*
to the concept of duty or debt that regulates justice in the social contract
and that equates ethics with "*rectitude* of address," what arrives as directly
as possible at "the place of essential decision" (1992a, 17). We have a
duty not to reduce responsibility to the form of a pro-positional response.
It is "*our duty above all* not to, approach in a direct, frontal *projective*, that

is, thetic or thematic way" (1992c, 11). And this recourse to the language of duty, our "duty above all not to," when it is our "duty above all not to" reduce to duty or debt, need not imply a "shortcoming," Derrida suggests. The shortcoming occurs when we cover over the way language of duty falls short. "Nothing could seem more violent or naive than to call for more frontality, more thesis or more thematization, to suppose that one can find a standard here" (11).

How then to conclude? We could say that deconstruction does not give us an ethics, an address of rectitude. And that to speak of an ethics of deconstruction, as Simon Critchley does, is not to claim that "*an* ethics can be derived from deconstruction," that an ethics has its origin or foundation in the deconstructing subject or self (Critchley 1992, 2; Bernasconi 1987). Derrida does not *come before us* as an authorial subject, and the "Come" is not his call. But we could also say that while deconstruction presents no new morality, it is not an amorality or an immorality, and it is not indifferent to questions of justice.[16] While perhaps "seeming" not to "address" these questions, Derrida "has done nothing but address [them], if only *obliquely*, unable to do so directly" (1992a, 10). The *elliptical* address is made necessary by the deconstructible structure to which deconstruction responds. Moreover for Derrida, as for Lyotard in the following chapter: "one cannot speak *directly* about justice, thematize or objectivize justice, say 'this is just' and even less 'I am just,' without immediately betraying justice" (10). Justice is an impossible yet-to-come (*à venir*) (27). And as such, justice is the possibility of deconstruction (15), the infinite demand to which—with its "no, it's not that, it's not so simple" (1989a, 19)—deconstruction responds.

In the meantime, *let us wait and see* (the refrain, an apostrophe perhaps, is repeated in Derrida's "Passions").[17] For at least as long as justice, "as the experience of absolute alterity" (1992a, 27), remains *something unrepresentable*, deconstruction will find its motivation in responding to the apostrophe, "Come," the "always unsatisfied appeal, beyond the given determinations of what we call, in determined contexts, justice, the possibility of justice" (21). And in responding, deconstruction will continue to go astray. As Derrida puts it in his Cerisy paper, "the coming is always to come" (1982b, 85).

2

Arrive-t-il?

> There is no presence. It comes too late.
> Lyotard, "Anamnesis of the visible, or candour"

Jean-François Lyotard's *The Differend: Phrases in Dispute* might not be a book. For the text, which Lyotard refers to in the preface (xv) as a "pile of phrases," consists of no more than a discontinuous series of numbered entries which are grouped into sections and interrupted by "Notices" on various philosophical works. The entries can be read sequentially, but also in any number of other ways since, as Lyotard also says in the preface, *The Differend's* tempo is not diachrony, the linear time of our time. This "open structure," where at each instance "a multiplicity of connections and sequences" is possible, "highlights and dramatizes ('performs')" (Carroll 1984, 7) the problem with which *The Differend* deals: the problem of writing or speaking *after*, that is, without any pregiven rules. To begin writing *after* is to begin in the middle of an open field, without a metadiscourse to predetermine the origin and end of a phrase. The stakes of writing *after* are in rules which remain to be found.

Through one of its meanings, *le différend* designates the *différence* or multiplicity that characterizes this open field, where the "post-structure" of a phrase (addressor, addressee, referent, sense) is not necessary or pregiven, thus where "all linkage between phrases is open," and where "there are many different possible ways of linking phrases" (1988b, 8). In another, related meaning, *le différend* suggests the excess or remainder of signification, "the unstable state and instant of language wherein something which must be able to be put into phrases cannot yet be" (1988a,

13). Since, as Lyotard puts it, there can be only one phrase at a time ("There are many possible linkings (or genres), but only one actual or current 'time' [*une seule 'fois' actuelle*]" [136]), every linking (every writing or speaking) occasions a *différend*. In every linking, "something 'asks' to be put into phrases, and suffers from the wrong of not being able to be put into phrases right away" (13). *Le différend* refers to this "forgotten" something which both precedes writing and is its remainder, and to which writing is *called* to respond. To begin *after* is to begin in search of rules for writing which is *passible* to *le différend*. What is it to write (paint, speak, etc.) in openness to difference (*différée*) or heterogeneity, so that "the self is essentially passible to a recurrent alterity" (1991b, 59)? What is it to write so that linearity loses its privilege, and so that the time of the present (each re-present-ation) exceeds the here-now (1988b, 7)? The *after* signifies not a chronological or sequential *post*, but *postponement*, writing as self-deferral (*différer*).[1]

To theorize postmodernism as a new age, Lytoard says, is to repeat a chronology that is thoroughly modern, and to repeat modern chronology ("a constituting time, the 'living present,' in the charge of a transcendental subject" [1988a, 73]) is to return writing to modernity's impassible subject. Modernity takes its subject to be the origin of writing rather than writing's construction. For Lyotard, however, the subject is not an entity that exists as such independently of a text. The subject is not pre-existent or pregiven, but is made in the process of writing, of thinking or speaking, of what, in *The Differend*, he calls "phrasing." His use of the word "phrase" is, in one sense, an attempt to free himself and his reader of the illusion of the ready-made subject: the assumption that language (speaking, writing) is a simple transmitter of meaning from one pre-existent subject to another; that writing is "a message passing from an addressor to an addressee both of whom are independent of it" (1988a, 11). No ready-made "I" takes its place *before* Lyotard's phrase.[2] What the term "phrase" suggests, rather, is the heterogeneity of the open field, "open 'space-time' in which there are no more identities but only transformations," and in which *le différend* arrives "both too soon and too late" to be grasped and held by a determinable subject (1988b, 31–32).

To begin without the transcendental illusion of the subject is to begin by taking for granted only the phrase, or rather, "phrases, in their hundreds and thousands" (1992, 42), each of which comes on the scene as the possibility of something, and someone, different. Only the phrase is given. This means that while "[i]t is necessary to link," to phrase and to make connections between phrases, "the mode of linkage is never necessary" (1988a, 29). The only rule with which phrasing begins is the rule that phrasing is not ruled by a pre-given rule: "to link is necessary; how to link is contingent" (29). The only necessity is the necessity of contingency, of "the gap" (1988b, 32) that separates one phrase from another and that leaves linking open and undetermined—that makes impossible the synthesis of heterogeneity into a uniform system or end. This contingency of linking, Lyotard says, is the condition of social justice. His hypothesis is that a just social order is not based on conformity, but is open to a diversity of subjectivities and modes of phrasing, "a patchwork of language pragmatics that vibrate at all times" (Lyotard and Thébaud 1985, 94), and not necessarily in tune one with the other. I will come back to this matter of dissonance, to the idea of a social community in which divers voices are not brought into unity, an idea which Lyotard attributes to none other than Kant, and that he relates, paradoxically, to the *Stimmung*, the euphonic harmony of Kant's *sensus communis*.

But we always begin in the middle. Before turning to Lyotard's discordant agreement with Kant, whom he reads, as it were, alongside Levinas and Freud, I will refer briefly to his reading, or perhaps I should say, his "rewriting" of modernity's two grand narratives of social justice, liberalism and dialectical philosophy. In "Rewriting Modernity," Lyotard explains his use of the prefix re- as an attempt to remove postmodernism, the issue of writing *after*, from the periodization of a pre- and a post-, a before and an after. Periodization, he says, "leaves unquestioned the position of the 'now,' of the present" (1991b, 24), and of the self-presence of the reading or writing subject. He says that for him, rewriting modernity does not signify a return to an origin, to a starting point from which to inaugurate a new age, a new periodization, free of the errors of the past, for such rewriting can be no more than "the repetition of what it rewrites" (29). Rather, he links the prefix re- to the German *durch* (journey [passing] through) of Freud's technique of "memorization," *Durcharbeitung*, or to the *ana-* (passing) of anamnesis, to suggest that rewriting modernity ("postmodernism") involves "the passing through of *trans-* or *per*-laboration," a procedure of *working through* or *working across* to something which is forgotten "before" representation or memory. The point of such rewriting is not to achieve a new synthesis or to arrive at a new destination, but to work through, "to pass beyond synthesis in general" (54). This movement of anamnesis is "what so-called 'French thought' has been calling *writing* for a long time," he says (55). It does not imply the discarding or "forgetting" of history, that is of historical texts, but neither does it imply holding these texts in the present, grasping them and exhibiting their virtues or crimes. Anamnesis rereads, thus rewrites, so as to elaborate "an 'initial forgetting' " (1992, 80).

Forgetting

Lyotard opens *Heidegger and "the jews"* by saying that he writes "the jews" in lowercase, in the plural, and in quotation marks, to indicate that it is neither a nation, nor a political, religious, or philosophical figure or subject, that he puts forward under this name. "The jews" should not be confused with real Jews, he says, for "the jews" is neither a concept nor a representation; indeed, "the jews" has never been presented and is not representable. The term testifies to what "has not been anything and is nothing" and yet what "must be remembered as something that never ceases to be forgotten" (3). What he means to suggest by "the jews," he says later in the book, is something akin to the Freudian *Nachträglichkeit*: "with 'the jews,' it is a question of something like the unconscious affect of which the Occident does not want any knowledge. It cannot be represented without being missed, being forgotten anew, since it defies images and words" (26).

Etymologically, *Nachträglichkeit* (*Nachträglich*: supplementary, subsequent, additional; *Nachträg*: supplement; *tragen*: carry, bear [as, a burden, a sorrow]) suggests a (deferred) supplementariness which is experienced as anxiety or burden. Citing Freud's texts on the unconscious and repression, Lyotard refers to an initial shock or excitation "that is not 'introduced'," that "affects but does not enter" the psychic apparatus, "a shock of which the shocked is unaware" since it precedes the conscious/unconscious division, and so "need not be 'forgotten,' repressed according to representational procedures" (12). The initial shock remains "outside" and "in excess" of representation, but its "effect" (what Freud calls "unconscious affect") is nonetheless "felt." Something "will make itself understood 'later'," Lyotard says. The shock that comes "before" will make itself understood "after," as a second terror, anxiety, or "feeling of a threatening excess" which, however, is "born of nothing that can be verified in the 'present' situation" and which thus will have to be located "outside the present contextual situation, imputed to a different site than this one" (13).[3] The initial "excess" remains "outside" representation, yet

"persists not so much at the limits but rather at the heart of representation," as something that every representation forgets, but that nonetheless is forgotten "before" memory and forgetting (5).

This "unsettling strangeness, which 'from the exterior' lies in
reserve in the interior" (13) of representation, is what Lyotard alludes to
with the expression "the jews."[4] Like Freud's unconscious affect, "the
jews" points to something that is unassimilable to the West's "phenomenological" consciousness and its before/after order of time; something its
representational systems have been unable to name, to contain and exhibit, and which, for this very reason, they never cease trying to forget.
"The jews," he says, "are within the 'spirit' of the Occident that is so pre-
occupied with foundational thinking, what resists this spirit; within its
will, the will to want, what gets in the way of this will; within its accom-
plishments, projects, and progress, what never ceases to open the wound
of the unaccomplished" (22). Lyotard does not intend to name this unnameable something by naming it "the jews." The term, he says, is like *le
différend*, only a negative sign or a nonfigure of the distress of representation, of something that representation misses, that has not been and cannot be named. And yet, more than is the case with *le différend*, "the jews"
cannot be separated completely from a specific referent or name, from
the Jews whom the West has identified with "the jews." Says Lyotard:
" 'The jews' are the object of a dismissal with which Jews, in particular,
are afflicted in reality" (3). Antisemitism is one of the ways in which
Western culture has tried "to bind and represent as much as possible—to
protect against—the originary terror, actively to forget it" (23). And the
Nazi extermination of the Jews was to have done away with "the jews"
once and for all, to have accomplished the removal of all traces: "The
solution was to have been final: the final answer to the 'jewish' question.
It was necessary to carry it right up to its conclusion, to 'terminate' the
interminable. And thus to 'terminate' the term itself" (25).

In one sense, *Heidegger and "the jews"* marks Lyotard's intervention
in a particular debate. The book was one of a number of French publications that followed the release of Victor Farías' *Heidegger and Nazism*. In
his text, Lyotard attempts to situate discussion of the "Heidegger affair"
within what he calls an economy of deferral. Such an analysis admits the
two faces of Heidegger—one being the importance of his thought, the
other his being implicated in Nazism—without concluding that if one is
true then the other is false. Lyotard attributes the latter logic to "the
prosecutor Farías," who "places himself deliberately and narrowly on the

terrain of facts," who "calls for merciless critical examination of the documents," and on this basis for the condemnation and dismissal of Heidegger (55–56). Farías eliminates the "intrinsic irregularity" of the Heidegger affair, Lyotard maintains. Farías contends that if one of two conditions is true, then the other must be false: if a great thinker, then not a Nazi; or if a Nazi, then not a great thinker. But this exclusionary logic, *either p or not-p, and if p, then not-p*, is itself a way of forgetting, of precipitating a foreclosure, and for Lyotard, closure "is the very nucleus of what is in question" in the Heidegger affair (55–56). "The affair happens to us in the manner of the *Unheimliche*, familiar and strange," he says (55). More than just inquiry into "Heidegger's Nazism" in the accusatory manner of a Farías, the affair raises "the question of what Heidegger's 'politics' bears of troubling and familiar strangeness"; what, both in Heidegger's engagement with the National Socialist Party and even moreso in his silence on the extermination, "emanates silently from an 'unconscious' and unproved affection, which thought can seek to approach only by defending itself against it"; and what, in Farías's presentation of the issue as a litigation to be regulated by a verdict, belongs also to the *Unheimliche*. "For the one and the other repeat, in their essence and in their effect on our thinking, a foreclosure that is constitutive of Western thought as philosophy and as politics. An unforgettable continues to forget itself, reiterates its forgetting, in Heidegger's 'politics' as in our politics regarding that 'politics' " (55–56).

It would be a mistake to read *Heidegger and "the jews"* as concerned solely with the Heidegger affair, then, or even as limited to what Lyotard calls the "geophilosophy" that renders the affair "*une affair 'française'*." Rather, through the issue of Heidegger's "politics" and of the "politics of publishing" which sensationalizes the Heidegger affair, the book raises the "question of what, today, preoccupies, troubles, and makes thought despair, as it did Heidegger fifty years ago" and as it has done throughout the tradition and thought of the European West: "A question of the always failed relationship of thought to what it lacks, to what it seeks, and what it misses when, in order to touch it and act it out, it overnames it" (74). Lyotard often resorts to this vocabulary of *touching* and *acting out* to suggest types of thought or writing that attempt a grasping (hands-on) exhibition, a staged demonstration (*monstrare*) or denotative presentation, governed by the intrigues of will. "Intriguing means not opening your hand, holding things in the present (*maintenance*)," he says (1989, 225). It means turning in on oneself and turning away from what thought misses, as he suggests happens in Heidegger's philosophical writings of 1927, which are "marked by the same terms" as the political texts of 1933–34 (1990, 71). Heidegger's engagement with Nazism cannot be deduced from the text of *Being and Time*, Lyotard says, and the book, in itself, is neither a Nazi nor a proto-Nazi work. But by opening *Dasein* "to the authentic future-as-coming-toward-itself" (69), *Being and Time* "allows" this politics as one possible destiny to which the *Volk* "is 'projected,' 'served' by the knowledge that is delivered to it by the rereading of its 'tradition' " (71).[5] In Heidegger's "Nazi" engagement, there is, Lyotard claims, both "an intrinsic consistency with the existential-ontological thought of *Sein und Zeit*" and an inconsistency which "consists in missing the deconstructive task of thought in various ways" (1993, 145). And the closure of deconstruction is "due to another *Stellung* [enframing], another *closure*, and another forgetting": Heidegger's deafness to the problematic of justice which governs his silence on the *Shoah* (146). For Lyotard, the filiation between existential-ontological thought and such a "politics of forgetting" extends beyond the Heidegger affair to the Greco-European philosophical tradition that Heideggerian thought deconstructs. Thus:

> If Heidegger is at *fault*, as Lacoue-Labarthe says, and if this fault is not simply a flaw in the rigor of thought, it cannot be assessed on the basis of an existential-ontological or poetic-deconstructive "installation." This installation forgets that the Forgotten is not (only) Being, but the Law. The difference that is incessantly forgotten is not only ontico-ontological, there is also the difference between good and evil, between justice and tort, no less elusive than ontico-ontological difference and, like it, always demanding reinscription. One can never settle accounts with the difference . . . the negative lesson that the "forgetting" of the *Shoah* by the great thinker of Being teaches us is that this Forgotten is not primarily Being, but the obligation of justice. (147)

The difference that is forgotten "before" thought is what summons thought as the obligation or call of justice, "not as that to which it has to answer (by representing it), but as that to which it is owed, before which it has to turn around and to stand up, questioning" (1990, 60). For Lyotard, it is as *Durcharbeitung* that writing responds to this call, as the process of working through that Heidegger attempted and that Lyotard, too, tries to practice in his episodic passings through modernity's metanarratives of social justice. In his reading, these master narratives are exclusionary systems, in the first place because they are organized around a sender-addressor and closed off from the heterogeneity of the addressee. The pole or post of the addressee is "forgotten, actively forgotten in Western thought," Lyotard says in *Just Gaming* (37), where he works through the discourse of liberal (Anglo-American) justice, the rhetoric of individual rights in which we are all immersed, as example of a justice that puts the subject first, before the law, as both its author and its judge. Liberal justice is based on the principle of autonomy, which says that "[o]ne is the author of the law that one pays heed to" and that the one who states the law "remains autonomous even when he obeys it since he is its author" (31). This assumption of the autonomous addressor relegates justice to the sphere of cognition, where writing is denotative exhibition, and where the addressor's autonomy is taken to guarantee the referentiality ("truth") of his or her presentations. The supposition of referentiality leads in turn to an assumed conformity between addressor and addressee, "a situation in which an author can write while putting himself at the same time in the position of a reader, being able to substitute himself for his own reader, and to judge and sort out what he has accomplished from the point of view of the reader that he also is" (10). In a justice of autonomy, the author knows for whom s/he writes, knows that the text is addressed to a subject identical to the one from whom it came. In a justice of autonomy, "the contour of an addressee is imposed" (10).

Through this I-you structure which "the moderns, whether consciously or not, held up as their ontological and political model" (1992, 27), a justice of autonomy closes itself off from any obligation that comes "before" it, and from any standard of legitimation other than that of its knowing and norm-giving subject (a standard it takes as given, rather than as made or imposed). It might be enough to say of this system, as Lyotard does, that "any attempt to state the law, for example, to place oneself in the position of enunciator of the universal prescription is obviously infatuation itself and absolute injustice" (Lyotard and Thébaud 1985, 99). But as in *Heidegger and "the jews"*, Lyotard's analysis of the problem in *Just Gaming* extends to the "capital issue of terror" (99), to the anxiety which he says traverses the social bond, and prompts autonomy's foreclosure of what it misses or lacks. The ideals of completion and control have allowed for the modern penetration of will into language, he says; and for the formation of a social contract comprising only like-minded addressors, a community resembling machines that "are built to lack nothing, except lack" (1993, 153).

The Differend, which moves from the "language games" of *Just Gaming* into the terminology of the linking of phrases, opens with several examples of cases where injustice occurs.[6] These are cases in which the rule of speaking, *either p or not-p, and if p, then not-p*, is formulated by an addressor before any speaking occurs. The cases illustrate what Lyotard considers to be the incommensurablity of justice with a system that subsumes obligation to a discourse of proof, and that dismisses (as "mystagogy," we might say) what cannot be presented by a cognitive phrase. Thus, for Lyotard: "As a general rule, an object which is thought under the category of the whole (or of the absolute) is not an object of cognition." Moreover: "If the requirement of establishing the reality of a phrase's referent according to the protocol of cognition is extended to any given phrase, especially to those phrases that refer to a whole, then this requirement is totalitarian in its principle" (1988a, 5). What matters is that questions of justice be freed from the hold of the cognitive, not in order that the questions be submited to the hegemony of another genre ("There is no genre whose hegemony over the others would be just" [158]), but in order that the contingency of linking be maintained: "To link is necessary, but a particular linkage is not" (80). A philosophy of justice might be called pre-scriptive, Lyotard says, insofar as it begins in the middle of an open field, "before knowing what to say and how to say it" and as such "is ahead of where it is supposed to be" (1992, 103); but not in the sense of a prescriptivism that pre-scribes writing's rules (is ruled by a pre-given rule). A philosophy of justice does not dictate a conformity between writing's addressor and its addressee. "That the engenderment of the rule be the stakes of the discourse (or, that one phrase in order to learn how one is able to phrase what one phrases) is the rule in the philosophical genre" (1988a, 97).[7]

Lyotard makes the latter remark in the "Result" section of *The Differend*, in a reading note on Hegel, where he argues that although dialectical philosophy presents itself as engenderment, as the engenderment rather than as the pretaking of phrasing's rules ("I am the very engenderment of the true in the linkings of phrases" [95]), and therefore as open to a heterogeneity which is external to the current phrase, it fails as philosophy precisely because it is ruled by nonderived rules.[8] "There are no true discussions" (86) within the dialectical genre, according to Lyotard, because it is as much ruled by the concept, and so by the presupposition of, and resolution into, sameness, as is the discourse of liberal justice. The dialectical Same is the *Selbst*, Absolute Being or Absolute Subject which, Lyotard says, both pre-exists the current phrase (and so functions as a rule that is applied "before" the phrase occurs) and is its pre-given end or "result." Dialectical linking takes place as "a movement which, by passing the *Selbst* [self] from the position of referent in the universe of an unmediated phrase to that of addressor and addressee in the universe of a phrase 'linking onto' the preceding one, in effect authorizes the second phrase" (89). This circulation of the *Selbst*, at once its negative *removal* from one phrase post to another, and its affirmative preservation or *raising* (93), culminates in the *Resultat*, an end which comes again and again: "This goal is incessantly attained and accordingly never attained. If it is attained, it is not attained. When it is not attained, it is still attained" (96).

Dialectical philosophy is entered on one condition, Lyotard says, "the initial displacement of the subject into a polymorphous *Selbst*" (96). This condition of the *Selbst* "is the presupposition found at the 'exit' which, according to the rule of the *Resultat*, is an entrance. There is one and only one X. It is the same under the various forms and throughout all the operations, and that it is why it is totalized into a single *Resultat*, which is disintegrated in turn for new operations" (96). But this presupposition of the same, "a rule that governs metaphysical discourse (as its closure)," is pre-given and not engendered: "Philosophical examination never reveals such a subject-substance. It reveals phrases, phrase universes, and occurrences, with, respectively, presentations, presenteds, and events" (96–97). Thus, like the discourse of autonomy, dialectical philosophy, in Lyotard's reading, admits no standard of legitimacy outside of its Subject-*Selbst*. This *Selbst* synthesizes different genres, and therefore different addressees, into one, Lyotard says, such that there is no outside to this philosophy, and such that, despite the preeminent place occupied by the we (the social, the community) in Hegelian dialectics, the collective "for us," in the moment of the *Resultat*, vanishes into the *Selbst*. The price paid for this philosophy "is the suppression of the we as an identity that thinks or phrases from the outside" (96).[9]

The principle of conformity which, in Lyotard's reading, informs both analytical and dialectical linking, leads to "the loss of the modern we" (1992, 30), to an uncanny foreclosure, a forgetting, of the heterogeneity, *le différend*, of the addressee. What modernity's two metanarratives of social justice name the we is only a vehicle of the transcendental illusion of the subject: the assumption of a permanent subject-substance that pre-exists phrasing and that "leaps from one instance situation to another" (1988a, 99). But "after Auschwitz," Lyotard says, this transcendental illusion can no longer legitimate a discourse of justice. What Lyotard, following Theodor Adorno, calls "Auschwitz," in quotation marks, designates a mode of phrasing for which there is no speculative *Resultat*. In the "Auschwtiz" mode, as Lyotard analyses it in *The Differend* (97–106), there is no linkage discoverable between two "unconjugatable phrases"—one, an order to die (*That s/he die, I decree it*), the other a sentence of death (*That I die, s/he decrees it*)—because there is no way of conjoining an I and a you into a third party we. "Auschwitz" signals an "unchainment," a suspension of the monopoly of the cognitive regimen of phrases. This unchainment is also "the interruption of the *Selbst*, its splitting apart" (106). It becomes necessary, "after Auschwitz," according to Lyotard, to find a principle for linking *otherwise* than in conformity with modernity's I-you rule of the Same: "The question raised by 'Auschwitz' is that of the genre of discourse that links onto 'Auschwitz.' If it is not the speculative genre, which one can it be? How does it authorize itself, if it is not thanks to the *Aufheben?*" (89).

Not remembering, but anamnesis

In *Just Gaming*, Lyotard recommends "the absolute privileging of the pole of the addressee, as the only site in which the social body can hold" (37). The remark is made in reference to Emmanuel Levinas, whose work, Lyotard says, "marks the place where something is prescribed to me, that is, where I am obligated before any freedom" (37). That obligation is *prior* to freedom means that *before* one speaks or writes, one is first of all spoken to, and that the position or authority of addressor of the obligation is never available for a speaker or writer to occupy. Thus, privileging of the pole of the addressee does not mean a simple change of places between an I and a you: it is not a matter of this or that forgotten addressee learning to write as an addressor; and neither is it a matter of an addressor learning to speak in the place of a forgotten addressee. For Lyotard, what is at stake in a discourse that privileges the addressee is what Levinas calls *passivity*: akin to anamnesis or *Durcharbeitung*, *passivity* suggests not a reversal but a *trans*-versal of the phrase-instances I and you.

Lyotard expands on these points in his reading note on Levinas in *The Differend*, where he considers passivity in Levinas' terms as consisting in the "ethical event" of an addressor's being addressed by, and made liable to, an other. Lyotard contends that this event of obligation cannot be conceived through Husserl's transcendental idealism or through the dialectical oppositions of Hegelian philosophy since, in Levinas' philosophy, the other who addresses the I is not *its other*, its concept, and since no self-conscious ego proceeds from the ethical event. "As scandal for the ego, the ethical relation presupposes two kernel phrases: *The ego does not proceed from the other; the other befalls the ego*" (110). Levinas emphasizes the asymmetricalness of the ethical relation, where there is no equivalency between the I and the other which would allow the other to be reduced to concept or self-identity, and where there is no way of conjoining the ethical to the sphere of cognition. The scandal of the event of obligation consists in the ego's radical displacement from the addressor instance, so that s/he can know nothing at all about the other whose addressee s/he is:

> The appearing of the other is not an event of cognition. But it is an event of feeling. The I, placed in the position of *you*, is someone to whom a prescription is addressed, the simple prescription that there be prescriptions (and not only descriptions, not only cognitions). The I in this situation learns nothing, since there is nothing to learn (a command is not a bit of information). The I does not even know if the other is also an I, nor does the I know what the other wants from the I nor even if the other wants something from the I, but the I is immediately obligated to the other. (111)

What breaks in on the ego in the ethical event is, in other words, *nothing but an apostrophe*: "the other is nothing but his or her request and my obligation" (111).[10] A messenger without a message, "the other, as an exteriority whose reason does not lie within the ego, announces the insufficiency of knowledge. The other announces no sense, it is the announcement, the non-sense" (110). It is this exteriority of obligation to cognition that prompts Lyotard to suggest (Lyotard and Thébaud 1985, 69) that, in Levinas' terms, the "game of the just" is played on the side of transcendence, but where transcendence is *empty*, without concept, and where the other remains *anonymous*: "the other in its destitution does not even have a name. He or she is not called, he or she is what calls"

(1988a, 112). Levinas' ethical event does not take place in the field of knowledge. Indeed, Lyotard says, "[i]t does not take place at all, since the other is not localizable . . . The ethical realm is not a realm, it is a mode of the *I/you* situation which happens unforeseeably as the scrambling of the phrase universe in which *I* is *I*" (112).

Something precedes what we call ethics or politics, then, something that happens (*il arrive*) as a displacement of the authorial I, and that, in so happening, "institutes a new universe," a phrase universe in which "an I [is] stripped of the illusion of being the addressor of phrases, grabbed hold of upon the addressee instance, incomprehensibly" (111). However, given the exteriority or priority of this event, the new phrase universe that it institutes cannot be presented by a phrase of cognition. The I, displaced onto the you instance by the ethical event, will return in the addressor's situation when another (cognitive) phrase is formed. In the subsequent phrase, as Lyotard puts it, "the I no longer understands anything about ethics, it is only able to believe that it understands. The passage from the ethical phrase to the phrase of knowledge is done only at the price of forgetting the former" (111). Thus, insofar as philosophy, including moral philosophy, consists in phrasing by concepts, it cannot not forget the event of the arrival of the ethical phrase. Writing *after* cannot present the unpresentable event that comes *before* it. Writing can, however, bear witness to the event through what Levinas calls *passivity*.

As "passive" or "transpicuous" to what comes "before" it, Levinas' own writing is "ethical," Lyotard suggests. Indeed, Levinas might be said to be engaged in the search that Lyotard refers to in *The Differend* as the search for new posts, "new addressees, new addressors, new significations, and new referents" (13), which would allow for an "ethical" response to what phrasing misses: *le différend* that "asks" to be put into phrases and that cannot be phrased. The need for new posts is brought up again in *Heidegger and "the jews"*, where the question Lyotard raises is not the question of whether or not to write, but rather the question of *how* to write so as not to forget "the jews," the unforgettable and always forgotten to whom Heidegger forgot to defer. "One *must*, certainly, inscribe in words, in images. One cannot escape the necessity of representing. It would be sin itself to believe oneself safe and sound," Lyotard says (1990, 26). What is in question is *how to write* so as not to continue forgetting. "Response (*répons*) rather than answer" (60) as the obligation of writing *after*: as in the writing of Levinas, where the goal is not to make the I master, but to work through to an event that the I cannot manage to think. In Levinas' texts, Lyotard says, "[i]nstead of being the description of an experience, conducted by an I in quest of self-knowledge . . . writing is the testimony of a fracture, of the opening onto the other . . . its aptitude for hearing a call (1988a, 113).

As the work of Levinas suggests, writing as response to the other turns the writer the other way around, even as it reverses the order which places modernity's subject before the law.[11] In Levinas' thought, Lyotard says, obligation does not result from an authority previously legitimated by an I or an us: "If I am obligated by the other, it is not because the other has some right to obligate me which I would have directly or mediately granted him or her. My freedom is not the source of his or her authority: one is not obligated because one is free, and because your law is my law, but because your request is not my law, because we are liable for the other. Obligation through freedom or consent is secondary" (112). Or, as Lyotard puts it in *Just Gaming*, obligation for Levinas "comes first and is much older, much more archaic" than freedom (35). To accept the obligation is to "remember" the pre-encounter with the other in post-encounter phrases (1988a, 112). This "memory" makes the subject an alien double, and it makes writing *after* an experience of exile:

> Levinas' "marvel" comes close to the "alienness" of the Gnostics, particularly in Marcion's case (Jonas 1958, 49–51). Obligation alienates the ego: it becomes the you of an absolutely unknowable other. Jonas also uses the word *Unheimlichkeit*, which gathers within itself the contradictory relation between ego and other. In acceding to the request, I go out far away from my home, as a hostage, without ever taking up habitation with you, nor ever being your guest, since you have no residence, but I also thereby fulfill my calling, which is to be at home no longer. (115)

In the same "Obligation" section in which he considers the work of Levinas, Lyotard introduces one of the four Kant notices that appear in *The Differend*. The statement with which this notice begins—"The law is not deduced" (118)—provides an indicator of why Kant, as well as Levinas, is important to Lyotard's understanding of ethics. In Kant, Lyotard says, he finds the "irreplaceable distinction" (Lyotard and Thébaud 1985, 85) between a prescriptive and a denotative phrase, between practical reason, which determines no intellectual content, and speculative reason, which proceeds by means of denotations. As he does with Levinas, Lyotard reads the Kantian distinction as granting priority and exteriority to a "prescriptive" or "ethical" phrase, such that a "prescriptive" is unrepresentable in a phrase of cognition. For Kant, as for Levinas, Lyotard says, "obligation is empty, in a way" (Lyotard and Thébaud 1985, 70), since it brings with it no determinant concept of justice, and since there is "no knowledge in matters of ethics" (73). And for Kant, as for Levinas, the priority of prescription implies a reversal of direction: the positioning of the law not as a conclusion of object-language but as its premise. "The Kantian argument is that prescriptive phrases, far from being regulated by principles like causality, on the same order as descriptive phrases, are themselves the cause of the acts they engender" (1988a, 119). In the Kantian analysis, then, the I comes "after" the prescription, as its addressee, rather than "before" it as its sender.

The Kant to whom Lyotard refers here is largely the Kant of the second *Critique*, and to the extent that Lyotard is a Kantian, he is so in relation to this Kant or to the Kant of the *Critique of Judgement*, and not to the Kant who forgets his own distinction between an Idea, what Lyotard calls a prescription, and a concept or a phrase of cognition (see Carroll 1987, 173f.). An Idea is not a concept, Lyotard insists. It has nothing "in common" with a description or a cognition. But Kant does not always respect this exteriority of the Idea. In his late writings, Lyotard says, Kant comes to take finality so seriously that the Idea of a "suprasensible totality" is identified with the social we, the totality of reasonable, practical beings. With this "return of the denotative in the very heart of Kant's prescriptive statements . . . both practical reason and political reason are still beholden, in Kant, to metaphysics" (Lyotard and Thébaud 1985, 85, 88). For Lyotard, an Idea cannot be presented, grasped or grabbed hold of by a philosophy of the concept, but the idea of the Idea is nonetheless the necessary precondition, the "transcendental condition," for any just philosophy of justice. This is what Lyotard reads both Kant and Levinas to suggest: that an Idea, an obligation, comes "before" the ego and the writing of ethics. This "fact" of obligation "has no consideration for self-love, kindness toward the self, self-satisfaction, or arrogance," Lyotard says. Thus the event of its breaking-in on the subject "does away with the presumptuousness of the self" (1988b, 36).

Despite its absolute exteriority, then, the event of obligation is not, in Lyotard's reading, an abstraction irrelevant to issues of social-political justice. Like Levinas' passivity, Kant's principle of analogy suggests that to phrase *after*, in openness to the Idea, is to represent *otherwise*. Kant's analogy is a negative mode of linking across the "impassible abyss" that separates a prescriptive from a cognitive phrase, "a mode of passage which is no longer simply the extension of a legitimation from one realm to another, but the establishment of a differential for the respective legitimations" (1988a, 123). The "as if" passage allows for similarities without hollowing out or filling in the abyss, Lyotard says: "The analogy resulting from the *als ob* is an illusion when the differences are forgotten and the differend smothered" (123). This negative *als ob* passage becomes particularly important when Lyotard turns to Kant's third *Critique*, and to aesthetic judgment, as the very principle of anamnesis or analogy itself. It is only the "as if," Lyotard suggests, which connects Kant's *sensus communis* and the social-communal we.

Sensus communis

In describing the faculty of judgment as a "middle term" between the faculty of knowledge and the faculty of desire, Kant's third *Critique* already grants feeling a synthesizing function as that which makes possible a linkage between understanding and reason, that which effects "a transition from the faculty of pure knowledge, i. e., from the realm of concepts of nature, to that of the concept of freedom" ([1790] 1958, 17). But at the same time, Kant is careful to distinguish the mediating faculty from the other two, so that, for example, although pleasure in the beautiful "is by the judgement of taste pronounced valid for every one," this universality or finality associated with feeling has nothing to do with cognitive judgement, "does not deal with any *concept*," and is "exclusive of any end (objective or subjective)" (62–63). The synthesis implied by the "universally communicable" (63) in the feeling of beauty is irreducible to cognitive or practical consensus, to an *end* of intellect or will. And by the same token, the determining ground of a judgment of taste cannot be the concept of an origin, for an aesthetic judgment "affords absolutely no (not even a confused) knowledge of the Object," Kant says, but rather "is called aesthetic for the very reason that its determining ground cannot be a concept, but is rather the feeling (of the internal sense) of the concert in the play of the mental powers as a thing only capable of being felt" (71). Lyotard will emphasize this point in his reading of the taste, the *sensus communis*, of which Kant speaks in *The Critique of Judgement*, particularly in section 40: that the universally communicable *sensus*, the feeling of the beautiful that must be declared in concert, in one single voice, admits of no concept of unified sender, and is not a matter of social consensus.

In his essay, "Sensus Communis: The Subject in *Statu Nascendi*,"[12] Lyotard points out that for Kant, taste (*sensus*) is a pleasure free of the mediation of either intellect or will. Given this, the common sense (*sensus communis*) of the third *Critique* cannot be *intellectio communis*, good sense or sound understanding; and even less can it be *intellectio communitatis*, the intelligence of the community: "It is a question of a community that is still—but that *still* presents a problem—unintelligent. Unintelligent, therefore, that is to say, proceeding without intellect. And unintellected, too, that is to say, one whose concept, *ex hypothesi*, will always be missed" (1991a, 217). As "ungraspable" by the concept, and as "disinterested," that is, free of the intrigues of will, the *sensus communis* implies a universality other than that of conceptual or cultural synthesis, Lyotard says, so that even using such a word as "universality" here is highly ambiguous. "For the cognitive community (the scientific one in its most determinate modality) these words 'necessity,' 'universality,' 'finality,' are names of categories that can be defined and exhibited, applicable in the space-time of experience" (218). But the common of the *sensus communis* is a judgment, "a 'state of mind,' that as yet owes nothing (nothing as yet, or already nothing) to knowledge and its intrigues" (219). It is a blind judgment, that is, "a judgement not having 'knowledge' of its end. . . . It has nothing whatever to do with an end or purpose. . . . So the finality, the purposiveness is end-less, purposeless, without a concept of its end. This is why the feeling of the beautiful has nothing to do with perfection, with this completion that the *Vollkommenheit* connotes" (220).

And yet, Kant's "go-between" faculty, while it has nothing to do with universality as project or purpose, does act *reflexively* on a certain *consensus*. There is an aesthetic synthesizing, Lyotard says, but only as a *Stimmung* " 'on the inside' of the subject, so to speak" (226), only as a feeling of internal euphony between the faculty of understanding and the faculty of imagination. In *Peregrinations*, Lyotard describes this feeling as the pleasure which the subject feels as a "result" of "the affinity between, on the one hand, the way its imagination works while it presents forms, rhythms, etc. on the occasion of perceiving an object and, on the other, the way its understanding *could* (and only *could*) operate on these forms to give them a conceptual rule" (30). Such agreement between the faculties is the necessary *a priori* condition of knowledge which, Kant says in Section 21 of *The Critique of Judgement*, would otherwise constitute "a mere subjective play of the powers of representation, just as scepticism would have it" ([1790] 1978, 83). Lyotard maintains in "Sensus Communis" that the agreement need not happen every time, it need only be possible: "Kant does not say that the said euphony is necessary to every piece of knowledge. He says that a proportion among the faculties is necessary for every piece of knowledge, and that it is necessary for one among all the possible proportions to be preeminently euphonious. It happens or it does not happen empirically, and with anyone. But it must be able to happen" (227).

Lyotard's argument is that, in order for there to be knowledge in general, there must be a preliminary *sensus* in action as much in understanding as in ethics, but that since this *sensus* is feeling, it cannot be touched by either intellect or will. The affinity can never be determined or predetermined, he insists, and it gives no matter, no position, to be programmed: "For if it were programmable, then the result would be an objective knowledge of the object, since knowledge is achieved with the actual subsumption of perceived matter under a category of understanding through the mediation of a schema" (1988b, 30). The affinity can only be felt, since it is "transcendental," or as Lyotard says in "Sensus Communis," since it comes *before*. It is a "judgement before the concept, and even before the schema, before the operation of a synthesis" (1991a, 219). It is "a kind of transcendental coenesthesia, which 'precedes' all diachronization. The agreements, the chords are only organized in a melodic line secondarily, through the organization of rhythm into diachronic time" (226). Lyotard's reading of Kant in "Sensus Communis" foregrounds the musical terminology of the third *Critique* to make the point that when Kant speaks of harmony or accord, his reference is to "an interior music" or "an intimacy of sounds," the voice, the *Stimme*, through which "the subject gives voice to itself 'before' it sees itself or conceives of itself" (226), that is, "before" it is positioned as a so-called subject.[13] The harmony is "relative merely to the relationships of the faculties with each other in the subject" (225), albeit in the subject which is not yet a subject. Thus Kant's harmony, in Lyotard's reading, cannot be understood as an accord of empirical individuals: "If there is a 'pragmatics', that is, an examination of sense in terms of its destination," he says, "then the senders and receivers in action in this destination, in this *Bestimmung*, are the constitutive instances of the supposed 'subject':

imagination, understanding, at least. And the *Einstimmung*, that would be the chorus made up by these voices" (225).[14]

And although the pre-subjective synthesis is the necessary condition for knowledge, and for the subject of knowledge, the mode of linking between the "before" and the "after" does not fill in the "impassible abyss." When pleasure in the beautiful is "put under house-arrest" by being projected onto an object we call beautiful, "this house-arrest is itself only analogical," Lyotard says (224). There is no way to exhibit the *sensus communis*. While the universality of the feeling of the beautiful is necessary if there is to be aesthetic judgment, what is declared "before" in one single voice cannot turn itself into a model, or provide the basis for a universality "after." Kant's *sensus communis* "is not a matter of social consensus, and even less of one obtained by ballot," Lyotard claims. "The beautiful does not get elected like Miss World" (225). Only analogy is permitted as a mode of passage between the "before" and the "after," only linkage which proceeds by means of "the mainspring of the *other*" (225). For Lyotard, this "going via the other" (228) relates to Kant's point that in matters of taste, both intellect and will are found lacking: in judgments of the beautiful, imagination presents forms which place it in agreement with understanding, but these forms, free of intelligence and without any possible interest, are in a relation of distant, or dissonant, "resemblance" to what comes "after":

> Indeed, the freer form is from concept, and thus independent of schematic structures the purer the euphony of the two faculties will be. Because it is not right, either, that form should be subsumed directly under the concept, for that belongs to the constitution of objectivity; but it is necessary for taste that form, however dissonant it is in relation to the concept, however much a stranger, in its free production, from what the understanding can regulate, should indicate, however (even in its dissonance), a possible task for the faculty of rules. And this is how form animates that faculty, one would like to say: that form provokes, excites the understanding. The dissonant agreement, lack of harmony do not scare Kant—on the contrary. (229)

The unison of the divers voices of the faculties "is even more enlivened" (231) when form puts intelligence in disarray. As Lyotard's reading would have it, taste is, as it were, a "deconstructive" judgment: on the one hand, an agreement, a harmony, and on the other hand, a discord, an operation of untuning. And in both respects, the "mainspring of the other" is at work. The "before" goes "via the other" because the *sensus communis* is reflexive and not determining: "the unity is not presupposed, it is a state of 'comparison,' a sudden pairing up of the faculties. This pairing up does not establish a parity, the parties are not a pair, they remain incomparable" (232). And the I that comes "after" this "go-between" goes "via the other" too, for "the aesthetical pleasure will always come along to disconcert it, to make it indeterminate, to make it be at a loss through its own concert, and its reflexive relation to itself" (233). The euphonious *sensus communis* can only *untune* the intellect, and the subject, once born, can "remember" ("make heard") the transcendental synthesis only by missing, or *forgetting* ("not hearing"), itself. The universality is "before" and not "after." It must be protected from all anthropologization, Lyotard says, even from the anthropologization given it by Kant.

The caution becomes particularly necessary, for Lyotard, where, in the third *Critique*, "the appeal—let us call it the appeal—for euphony is described, the summons, the *Ansinnen* and the wait, the promise of euphony" (227). Rather than reading the appeal to the other contained in the beautiful as "directed by an inclination to society" (a reading, he notes, against which Kant protests in section 41), Lyotard takes this appeal to the other to be a "going via the other" of deferral or dissonance, such that the *sensus* and the community remain separated by an abyss across which there is only an "as if" passage. Indeed, it is at precisely the point where the appeal, the apostrophe, is "heard" that Lyotard, following Kant, would locate the breaking-in of an Idea of reason, and so the "transition" from an aesthetics of the beautiful to an aesthetics of the sublime. With this transition to the sublime comes a break-down of the "before-after" passage altogether. Kant's Idea of community is manifested where the imagination, required to present forms which would re-present the *sensus communis*, fails in its task, Lyotard says; where the mind finds itself lacking in imaginative forms: "The Idea, especially the Idea of pure practical reason, Law and freedom, is signalled in a quasi-perception right within the break-up of the imagination and therefore just as much via a lack or even a disappearance of nature understood in this way" (1991b, 137). The feeling of the sublime, then, "is none other than the sacrificial announcement of the ethical in the aesthetic field. Sacrificial in that it requires that imaginative nature (inside and outside the mind) must be sacrificed in the interests of practical reason" (137).

With this sacrifice of the imagination in the sublime (which, Lyotard says, owes nothing to the *sensus communis*), judgment is no longer simply the feeling of pleasure, but now the contradictory "faculty of pleasure and pain" (1991a, 222). And the pain (what Lyotard, following Burke, sometimes calls the "terror") is a "result" of the event of obligation, the break-in of an Idea of reason: "The entrance of suffering into esthetic feeling must be understood as a shadow cast over imaginative work by an Idea of reason" (1988b, 40). In that it introduces this terror, this "aesthetics of shock, an anaesthetics" (1990, 31), the Kantian sublime is, for Lyotard, "analogous" to the Freudian unconscious affect and to the deferred action of the *Nachträglichkeit* (31). In the sublime, some "shock" affects but does not enter the mind, something which overflows or excises the border or framework placed over the manifold by the imagination: "an 'excess' has 'touched' the mind, more than it is able to handle. That is why the sublime has no consideration for form, why it is an 'unform' " (32). And that is why, Lyotard says, the sublime, like the unconscious affect, renders the mind *infans*. The sublime belongs to an *infancy* "which would not be a period of the life cycle, but an incapacity to bind a certain something" (17).

We may be approaching Lacan and Kristeva here, with this "idea" of an "infancy" that is not a developmental period but an unrepresentable dimension of "thought." And notwithstanding the differences between Derrida's and Lyotard's readings of Kant, this *infans* may also suggest the *unrepresentable something* that Derrida associates with the supplement or trace; the unlocalizable something that he, like Lyotard, gives so many non-names. For both Derrida and Lyotard, this something that "remains 'within' the apparatus as its outside, infuse and diffuse" (Lyotard 1990, 32) "breaks-in" as obligation or call. For Lyotard, the event of the apostrophe can be read into what Kant calls the sublime or what Levinas calls hostage-taking. In the event of the apostrophe, a speaker-writer is addressed, before, by an other, asked to listen, but according to an "exhorbitant law of listening to the inaudible" (22). The voice that calls cannot spare the one who listens "the despair of never hearing what the voice says" (22). This is a "strange" aesthetics, Lyotard admits (1988b, 41).[15] It is an aesthetics *perversely inhabited by ethics*, but where ethics is no longer, or not yet, the purview of an addressor-subject.

PART TWO

3

Soulmorality

SPEAKING OF LOVE

*For, in psychology, objectification is subjected in its
very principle to a law of* méconnaissance *that governs
the subject not only as observed, but also as observer.
That is to say, it is not about him that you have to
speak to him, for he can do this himself, and therefore,
it is not even to you that he speaks. If it is to him that
you have to speak, it is literally of something else, that
is, of something other than that which is in question
when he speaks of himself, and which is the thing that
speaks to you, a thing which, whatever he says, would
remain forever inaccessible to him, if in being speech
addressed to you it could not elicit its response in you
and if, from having heard its message in this inverted
form, you could not, by returning it to him, give him
the double satisfaction of having recognized it and of
making him recognize its truth.*

Lacan, Écrits: A Selection

Writing to his fiancée Martha Bernays in 1883, Freud recounts his discovery in a "chapel-like room" of the Dresden art gallery of a Madonna
by Raphael, "a crowd of people in silent devotion in front of her" (1970,
97). Himself one of the spectators, Freud is disappointed with the
Dresden Madonna. "The painting emanates a magic beauty that is ines-
capable," he writes to Martha, "and yet I have a serious objection to raise

67

against the Madonna herself" (97). For what Freud sees in Raphael's Mary, instead of a heavenly virgin-mother, is a "nursemaid, not from the celestial world but from ours" (97). In gazing on the woman, Freud feels "a lack of satisfaction," John Forrester suggests, "that lack against which masculine sexuality characteristically defends itself by splitting the woman into two, the nursemaid and the mother, the whore and the virgin. As he put it in a letter to Fliess in 1898, 'In all analyses, one therefore hears the same story twice: once as a fantasy about the mother; the second time as a real memory of the maid' " (Forrester 1984, 4).

It seems appropriate, somehow, that Freud first "began to admire" painting (1970, 96) by viewing the Christian Madonna, for what representation has better performed the historical splitting of woman? And what representation, by performing this splitting, has better delivered unity, and therefore authority, to the on-looking male? By enshrining the biological integrity of the Virgin Mother (*ante partum*, *in partu*, and *post partum*), Christianity effectively elevated her idealized body beyond the realm of the flesh, so that "although Mary was surpassing fair," as Jacobus of Voragine puts it in his thirteenth-century *Golden Legend* (152), "no man could ever look upon her with desire." But the other side of this veneration of the sublime body of the Virgin is an abjection of the woman's body as flesh.[1] If not the impossible Mary, then Eve, the temptress "once fallen and forever after prone" (Kraus 1967, 46), Christianity's woman is irrevocably split, her body the object of either the upward or downward gaze of a masculine spectating subject.[2] And whether Freud stands in the Dresden gallery before the drawn curtains of Raphael's Mary or in a Viennese medical theater before a prostrate hysteric, one does seem to hear the same story twice, in psychoanalysis as in Christianity, the same binary model of sexual difference: male as observing subject; female as object, split into virgin or whore.

The consensus seems to be that one hears the same story again from Lacan. No more than Freud was Lacan "able to fathom the 'dark continent' of female sexuality" Alice Jardine writes in *Gynesis* (161). Lacan managed to "tak[e] psychoanalytic theory further than anyone before him," she says, but like Freud, he "never moved beyond the *male subject* as absolute metaphor" (161). And by interesting himself, like Freud, in women, Lacan "even repeated, strangely, Freud's itinerary" Jardine suggests: "The Papin Sisters, Saint Teresa, Marcelle, Aimée, Hadewijch d'Anvers, right up to the 'lady analysts,' all provided the bodies for Lacan's theoretical metonymy" (160–61). No text is more regularly cited to exemplify this "strange repetition-in-Freudian-syntax" (161) than Lacan's 1972–73 *Seminar XX, Encore.* Juliet Mitchell and Jacqueline Rose (1982, 137) describe this seminar as Lacan's "most direct attempt to take up the question of feminine sexuality, not just as part of a return to the earlier debate, but in a way which goes beyond Freud." Yet they also point out that *Encore* is one of Lacan's most difficult and polemical texts, often "accused of being complicit" (137) with the phallic sexuality which it tries to expose.

This complicity has been said to begin right with the seminar's cover, which bears a photograph of Gianlorenzo Bernini's marble sculpture *Ecstasy of Saint Teresa,* centerpiece of the Cornaro chapel of Santa Maria della Vittoria in Rome. Particularly considering the sculpture's setting, can the photographic reproduction do anything but reproduce Christianity's model of sexual difference? Bernini designed the entire Cornaro chapel as a theater for this sculpted altarpiece, even to the point of mounting *loggia* on the chapel's side walls. Positioned in these theater-boxes are male spectators, members of Cardinal Frederico Cornaro's family, cast in marble relief. On the stage, illuminated by shafts of light which descend from a chimney-like opening above, Teresa is recumbent, her languid body draped on marble clouds, her bare left hand and foot fallen limply at her side. Seemingly drawn forward by an angel's golden arrow, her upper body is raised; her luminous face, at once blissful and suffering, has lips parted, nostrils distended, eyes almost closed. In the words of one of Teresa's contemporary biographers (Lincoln 1984, xxxviii), the sculpture is a "sexually loaded . . . masterpiece," not only the carving of a celestial virgin, but "the world's only beautiful depiction of a woman in orgasm." In having a photograph of the sculpture grace the seminar cover, can Lacan do other than position himself in the *loggia,* then, among the members of the Cornaro family, another masculine spectating subject who sees the Bernini sculpture as representing the division of sex?

At issue in readings critical of *Encore* is not only Lacan's use of the photograph but also the text of the seminar itself, notably his oft-quoted remark that "c'est comme pour Sainte Thérèse—vous n'avez qu'à aller regarder à Rome la statue du Bernin pour comprendre tout de suite qu'elle jouit, ça ne fait pas de doute. Et de quoi jouit-elle? Il est clair que le témoignage essentiel des mystiques, c'est justement de dire qu'ils l'éprouvent, mais qu'ils n'en savent rien" (1975, 70–71). Stephen Heath translates *jouir* in the Lacan passage by the verb "to come" ("you have

only to go and look at the Bernini statue in Rome to understand that
[Teresa is] coming, no doubt about it. And what is she enjoying, coming
from? It's clear that the essential testimony of the mystics is that of saying
that they experience it but know nothing about it") and promptly ac-
cuses Lacan of assuming "the assurance of the position of knowledge"
(Heath 1978, 52). What is striking in the Lacan passage, Heath says,

> is the certainty in a representation and its vision (the cover of
> the book of the seminar is provided by a full-page photograph
> of the sculpture). No doubt, not the trace of any difficulty, to
> see the Bernini statue is to understand at once, is to have one's
> gaze filled with Saint Teresa's coming, with the *jouissance* of the
> woman; the statue is adequate, the image it gives enough. (52)

What Lacan sees in the sculpture is clear enough to Heath, because
Heath is certain that Lacan sees the sculpture as representing something
to be seen, that is, as a representation on the stage of the Cornaro chapel
of the inaugural scene of the phallus. The scene is the drama of discovering that visiblity is on the side of the man ("seeing is from the male
organ" [54]), Heath says, and that the woman, who does not have it
("seeing is understanding . . . that she has nothing to see" [53]), can only
be "the difference of the man, his term" (53). This discovery does not
divide the man, who is and remains one, an identity, but it defines the
woman, by virtue of her visibly lacking body, as divided and different, "a
difference in nature *to be seen*" (55). Heath insists that "Lacan instates
the visible as the condition of symbolic functioning;" that for Lacan, the
psychoanalytic positioning of the signifying subject "is brought down to a
matter of sight" (54). Thus the image of Teresa on the cover of *Encore*,
"the sureness of the religious representation, the woman held as the truth
of that view" (61): the truth is that certainty belongs to the man, and
that "[t]he something more, the *en plus*, that Lacan sees so readily in the
statue as the *jouissance* of the woman makes up for the something less, the
absence, that the woman represents, represents in the first instance according to a scenario that is another certainty of seeing" (53).

"Commenting on a text," Lacan says, "is like doing an analysis"
(1988a, 73). The question that motivates his life-long commentary on
Freud, *"what do we do when we do analysis?"* (10), might then also be the
question, *what do we do when we do textual commentary?*, that is, *what is it
to write or to read?* I will suggest in what follows that in both the analytic
scenario and in the situation of textual commentary, what matters most

to Lacan is not the visible, as Heath and others contend, but the unseen and nonrepresentable. To use Lacan's words: "In every analysis of the intersubjective relation, what is essential is not what is there, what is seen. What structures it is what is not there" (224). For Freud, analysis of dreams is preeminently the way to encounter this unseen and unsayable, this "what is not there" that structures the text. *The Interpretation of Dreams*, Lacan says (9), "is always, endlessly, about technique" (*what do we do when we do analysis? what do we do when we write or read?*). It may be significant to note then, in considering Lacan's choice of the photograph for the cover of *Encore*, that in the *Ecstasy of Saint Teresa*, Bernini casts the text of a dream. The dream is recurrent, and is described by Teresa in her autobiography (1946, 193) as that moment of transverberation when an angel with an flaming golden arrow pierced her heart repeatedly "so that it penetrated to my entrails" with a pain "so sharp that it made me utter several moans" and with such excessive sweetness caused by the pain "that one can never wish to lose it." Using the same nuptial imagery that is adopted by the other mystics mentioned in *Encore*—Bernard of Clairvaux, Hadewijch d'Anvers and John of the Cross—Teresa refers to this dream as the climax of her "spiritual marriage" to Jesus. "These mystical ejaculations are neither idle prattlings nor mere verbiage, indeed they are the best things you can read," Lacan says in *Encore* (1975, 71). But what do we do when we read these dream texts? *What is it to write or to read?* I will suggest that what is essential, for Lacan, is not the seen (the phallic scene) of representation, but rather "what is not there," and what, in not being there, performs representation's failure or lack.

As in the text, so in the analytic encounter, "what is not there" includes the analyst him- or herself. Lacan breaks with the therapeutic model of psychoanalysis by vacating the place or position of certain knowledge. In the analytic situation, he says, the analysand, seeking certainty for himself, transfers certainty onto the analyst. If the analyst returns certainty to the analysand by speaking from the place of the subject-supposed-to-know (*sujet supposé savoir*), then analysis functions only to confirm a certain subjectivity in both analyst and analysand. It's up to the analyst to break this circle of the self, Lacan maintains. It's up to the analyst "not to be there" (1988b, 246) in the place of certainty where s/he is expected to be. It's up to the analyst to be absent from the place of the Other in which s/he will be addressed. Heath charges Lacan with positioning himself in this place of certainty, but as Jane Gallop remarks, Heath's commentary on *Encore* returns a certain subjectivity to Heath. In *The Daughter's Seduction* (51),

Gallop questions Heath's "surprisingly confident" translation of *jouir* in the celebrated Lacan passage, a word which, she notes, Heath specifies elsewhere (in his translator's introduction to Roland Barthes' *Image Music Text*), as lacking a suitable English equivalent.[3] Gallop argues that Heath's translation "reimplicate[s] him in the 'confidence of knowledge' he is working to expose" in Lacan. " 'No doubt about it, not the trace of a difficulty,' Heath complains of Lacan's vision of Teresa's *jouissance*. Yet Heath's own lack of doubt is precisely his difficulty," Gallop writes; "his difficulty is a return of a phallic representation of self." That the circular return is not altogether successful indicates that Lacan is not in the place of certainty where Heath expects him to be. Heath asks: "Yet who exactly is Lacan addressing? Men? Women? Whose is the certainty he assumes so easily ('you only have to')?" (52), implying by his question that Lacan ought to have specified *exactly*, either the (sexual) identity or difference of his addressee. But the Lacan "passage is indifferent to such questions," Heath concedes, "as is Lacan's work generally." Lacan, for whom "the position of the analyst must be that of an *ignorantia docta*" (1988a, 278), does not know to whom his text is sent.

My interest in *Encore* is primarily an interest in the relation of psychoanalysis to ethics, a question which Lacan takes up in this seminar as well as in two earlier seminars, *Seminar VII* (1959–60) and *Seminar XI* (1964). I turn now to a consideration of what Lacan says about the question in these earlier seminars, and to how what he says links the question to his indispensable and variable theory of *le stade du miroir*. I will come back to *Encore* and the mystics, and to the "what is not there" that I take to be at stake in Lacan's contention that "The status of the unconscious . . . is ethical" (1977b, 33).

The Analytic Trope

> He speaks—to his patients, to the members of his
> School, to the seminar's audience, a bit everywhere.
> Such, he says, is his profession as an analyst. He turns
> this speaking into a way of withdrawing. It is the very
> act of his theory, the gesture which formulates this
> theory; it is also a lifetime's paradox. He attracts
> because he withdraws. Departures are scattered
> throughout his career.
>
> de Certeau, *Heterologies*

I shall begin where Lacan begins at one of the points of disruption that punctuate his life and work. *Seminar XI* (translated as *The Four Fundamental Concepts of Psychoanalysis*) opens on 15 January 1964 following his expulsion from the Société française de psychanalyse. It is the first of a new series of seminars at the École Normale Supérieure where Lacan faces a different audience than he did at the Hôpital Ste. Anne. Before the move, Michael Clark points out, Lacan's audience had been composed mostly of psychoanalysts, but at the École Normale Supérieure, "his audience broadened to include a wider range of the French intelligentsia, and the seminars also began to range more widely in philosophical topics" (Clark 1988, 73). The disparate audience signals a "deterioration," Michel de Certeau suggests: "Into the hall of the École Normale Supérieure, which provides a theater for the proceedings after 1964, the audience spreads, grows, overflows, increasingly beyond control. The 'proper' place, i.e., the École, fills up with anybody and anything" (de Certeau 1986, 48–49). The administration will not long tolerate this "dirtiness," de Certeau points out, and by 1968 will use "the physical disorder as a pretext to banish the intellectual disorder" (49). Lacan, the ex-centric analyst, will be displaced again, at issue in his ongoing controversy with the orthodox psychoanalytic establishment not only his tampering with received wisdom concerning such matters as the training of analysts and the length of the analytic session, but chiefly, the "intellectual disorder" implied in his concept of the unconscious subject.[4]

It is to this, the most fundamental concept of psychoanalysis, that Lacan turns in *Seminar XI*, suggesting, paradoxically enough, that the lineament of the concept of the unconscious can be found in the *Discourse on Method*: for "Descartes tells us—*By virtue of the fact that I doubt, I am sure that I think*," indicating that doubt, something in the beyond of consciousness, is the basis or ground of his certainty; and in a similar way, "Freud, when he doubts—for they are *his* dreams, and it is he who, at the outset, doubts—is assured that a thought is there, which is unconscious" (1977b, 35–36). At the point of doubt, the approaches of Descartes and Freud converge. On the point of certainty, however, their approaches take opposite directions, for Descartes, through what Lacan describes as the "handing back of truth into the hands of the Other, in this instance the perfect God" (36), seeks a place for the subject absolutely outside of language, while Freud, whose "subject is 'at home' in this field of the unconscious" (36), declares the certainty of that field, and pledges to seek the subject there, in the dream: "Freud says, *Whatever it is, I must go there.*

... There is the country where I shall take my people" (33). Lacan adds: "I am not being impressionistic when I say that Freud's approach here is ethical" (34).

The matter of doubt, which for Lacan is the matter of the unconscious, raises the issue of the relation between psychoanalysis and ethics, an issue with which he has wrestled before. He struggles with the issue but does not resolve it in his 1959–60 *Seminar VII, L'éthique de la psychanalyse*. Lacan hesitated to publish *Seminar VII*, Tobin Siebers suggests, because "[h]e seemed to fear that it was incomplete, an idea already expressed in the opening statement of the seminar where he decided to leave open the question of knowing what would be included under the topic" (Siebers 1986, 323–24). And when Lacan turns again (*encore*) to the subject of ethics in his 1972–73 *Seminar XX, Encore*, he continues to express uncertainty, his want of knowing something, or his want to know nothing (*rien savoir*), about it. Lacan opens *Seminar XX* by remarking that he did not publish *L'ethique de la psychanalyse* because "[w]ith time, I realized that I could say a little more about it. And then, I perceived that what was directing my progress was of the order of the *I want to know nothing about it* (*je n'en veux rien savoir*)" (1975, 9). From *Seminar VII* to *Seminar XX*, then, Lacan himself takes a different direction from the one followed by Descartes, and in so doing diverges not only from the psychoanalytic establishment but also from an entire tradition of metaphysical philosophy as, in accompanying Freud ("We are not following Freud, we are accompanying him" [1988a, 120]), he comes to locate the subject of ethics not in the realm of Law or conscious reason (rational mind in control of an appetitive body), but in the field of unconscious *jouissance* (see Lacan 1986, 252).

This *jouissance* is not the repressed (sexual) content of a dream. The unconscious is not the dream, Lacan says in *Seminar XI* (1977b, 37). Rather, the unconscious is "something other" (24) which makes itself felt through gaps or failures in the represented or recounted dream text, "that which marks, stains, spots, the text of any dream communication—*I am not sure, I doubt*" (35). Freud refers to this point of discontinuity as the *navel* of dreams, a term which, Lacan says, designates the "ultimately unknown centre" of dreams, and which like the anatomical navel, manifests itself as a hole or a gap in the dream-text (23). Lacan terms the point of discontinuity the "colophon of doubt," where the colophon refers to the small pointing hand that used to be placed in the margin of a typographic manuscript (44). "The colophon of doubt is part of the text"

(44). Indeed, he says, Freud not only includes doubt as part of the text, he underlines it: "Doubt . . . in his way of looking at it, is almost an *emphasis*—there is no equivalent word in French, one would have to say *soulignage*" (1988b, 126). Freud emphasizes the colophon of doubt because through it "something other" is for a moment brought into the light: "there is a hole, and something that oscillates in the interval" (1977b, 22). Something else appears in the gap, and this something else is the Freudian unconscious: "Impediment, failure, split. In a spoken or written sentence something stumbles. Freud is attracted to these phenomena, and it is there that he seeks the unconscious. . . . What occurs, what is *produced*, in this gap, is presented as *the discovery*" (25).

The unconscious is not the dream. It is not some negated content, scene or event, "the non-conscious, the more or less conscious, etc.," of which, Lacan says, there are "hundreds of additional varieties," including the Jungian romantic unconscious and "the hold-all heteroclite unconscious that Edward von Hartmann spent his life elaborating" (1977b, 24). All of these theories imply "that at the level of the unconscious there is something at all points homologous with what occurs at the level of the subject" (24), and all of them lead thereby to the practice of psychoanalysis as cure. Lacan opposes the therapeutic model of analysis because its work of curing the patient is a work of "stitching up" (23) the gap. Where the *un* of the unconscious, the *Un* of Freud's *Unbewusste*, has been associated with the idea of unity (the French *un*: one; the German negative *un*: negation), Lacan aligns it instead with the notion of *lack*: "Let us say that the limit of the *Unbewusste* is the *Unbegriff*—not the non-concept, but the concept of lack" (26). Where orthodox analysis aims at reintegrating the patient, Lacanian analysis endeavors instead to open up "the problematical relation of the subject to himself" (1988a, 29).

This problematical relation first emerges at the stage of the mirror. In his early works, Lacan discusses the mirror stage as a developmental moment which actually *takes place*.[5] According to this account, the would-be subject, at some time between the ages of six and eighteen months, *identifies* its self with the "ideal unity" and "unruffled surface" (1977a, 15, 19) of its specular body-image. The moment is one of fundamental misrecognition (*méconnaissance*), in that the coherence of the image is utterly discordant with the child's motor incoordination at this still-*infans* stage. But the misrecognition is nonetheless constitutive of the child as ego, formative of its self-conception as a unified and separate self. For it is just at this "moment" that the child begins to use language, learning to vest the specular "I" with positionality ("I am") in signification so that, as Kristeva puts it (1984d), "the specular image is the 'prototype' for the 'world of objects.' Positing the imaged ego leads to the positing of the object, which is, likewise, separate and signifiable" (46). The narcissism and aggressivity of the mirror stage are repeated each time the child takes its place as a unified subject within the sociolinguistic ("symbolic") system which Lacan calls the *Law* or *Name-of-the-Father (le Nom-[non]-du-père)*. Through signification, then, the *Law-of-the-Father's* binary order of difference is incorporated as the structure of subject identity. According to Lacan, this order of difference (subject/object, male/female, mind/body, same/different, present/absent, self/other, etc.) is nothing more than a construct in service of the imaginary "I" and its transcendent ("phallic") position. And yet, however arbitrary, this binary law makes the matter of subject positioning in relation to an image also a matter of the either/or ordering of (sexual) difference.

In that the myriad elements of "the problematical relation of the subject to himself" carry over, as it were, from the mirror stage to the stage-drama of signification, Lacan's mirror stage myth,[6] rather than providing the psychoanalytic interpretation *of* a diachronic-developmental event, may be said to describe the drama of signification *as* an event of spatial identification-splitting which is reenacted each time a signifying subject constitutes itself in the place of the Other. Rather than designating a genetic "moment" or a developmental "turning point," *le stade du miroir* suggests a synchronic turning, the signifying subject's repeated, infatuated *turning toward* imaginary unity, thus also simultaneously, its aggressive *turning away* from heterogeneity or difference. The subject is repeatedly "born" and "reborn" in this turning, this narcissistic identification with an image whose otherness-alterity is overlooked.[7] Samuel Weber suggests, however, that despite the effort to ignore it, "such alterity can never be entirely effaced, since it is what permits the identification to take place" (13). The specular subject is caught in a future anteriority: "it is only the *anticipated* motor and mental unity, visibly represented in the perception of the image and still wholly lacking in the child, which allows the mirror image, so crucial for the constitution of the ego, to have its effect" (13).[8]

This future anteriority of the mirror stage trope distinguishes Lacan's specular subject, characterized by "*anticipated belatedness*" (Weber 1991, 10), from the conscious subject of metaphysical philosophy, Hegel's *Selbst*, for example, whose basis is a perfected present. "In invoking the future anterior tense," Weber says, "Lacan troubles the perfected closure of the always-already-having-been [*des Immer-schon-gewesen-Seins*] by inscribing it in the inconclusive futurity of what will-always-already-have-been [*Immer-schon-gewesen-sein-wird*], a 'time' which can never be entirely remembered, since it will never have fully taken place. It is an irreducible remainder or remnant that will continually prevent the subject from ever becoming entirely self-identical" (9). This means that the positioning of onself as a unified ("phallic") subject within the *Law-of-the-Father* is an endeavor which inevitably fails. Aware of this failure, yet always attempting to cover it up, the signifying subject is beset by an inexorable anxiety, a disconcerting after-effect, an unrepresentable, contaminating and impossible to integrate, "*after the fact [après coup], nachträglich*" (1988a, 191) effect. For Lyotard, this *after-effect* bears such non-names as "the jews" and *le différend*. Lacan calls it *jouissance*.

"There never is a subject without an ego," Lacan submits (1988b, 246). It cannot, therefore, be the aim of psychoanalysis to do away with *le stade du miroir*'s specular drama. Analysis is not a matter of eliminating the subject's imaginary relation to the Other, he says, "but of having the subject assume it where it is" (246). This is what, for Lacan, makes analysis ethical: it endeavors to break the circular return of phallic identity by having the analysand come to realize that when s/he addresses the analyst as a subject of certainty, it is the Other that s/he is addressing; moreover, that in addressing the Other, something other is in question in the analysand him- or herself. Psychoanalysis consists in having the subject "become conscious of his relations, not with the ego of the analyst, but with all these Others who are his true interlocutors, whom he hasn't recognized," Lacan says (246). "It is a matter of the subject progressively discovering which Other he is truly addressing" (246). Insofar as "the analyst is not a living mirror, but an empty mirror" (246) of the unity-certainty that the analysand seeks, analysis, so understood, functions to *undercut* rather than *instate* the visible. Its goal is to open the subject (both analyst and analysand) to the *méconnaissance* at the root of the ego—as well as to something other with which the ego does not coincide.

To call this approach to analysis ethical is obviously not to imply that Lacanian analysis conforms to traditional ethics. Indeed, Lacan suggests in *Seminar VII* (28–35; 244–45) that traditional ethics is much like the orthodox analysis that he rejected, for both aim at "stitching up" the gap in the subject. In the Aristotelian tradition, he says, and continuing into modern moral philosophy from Descartes through Kant, ethics, like orthodox psychoanalysis, performs a therapeutic function: it offers the subject a way, a path (*la voie*), to realization of the self in the Other (the Sovereign Good, God, wholeness, happiness, autonomy, etc.). The direction, the path (*la voie*) of traditional ethics, leads the subject to assume an identification with the imagined ideal. Traditional ethics thus functions as sublimation, as an elevating of the object to the status of the Thing ("*L'objet est ici élevè à la dignité de la Chose*"), and as a collapsing of the distinction between what Freud called the realm of things, *die Sache*, and the Thing, *das Ding* (1986b, 133–34). As Lacan understands it, the path (*la voie*) of ethical analysis diverges from the path of morality. Indeed, he says in *Seminar VII* that Freudian analysis implies an "overturning," a "turning-around" (*renverser*), of traditional ethics (85). Analysis implies a *change in direction*, for what it takes to be the ethical question, "Have you lived in accordance with your desire?" ("*Avez-vous agi conformément au désir qui vous habite?*") (362), requires the subject's *re-turn* to the unconscious, to the remainder called *jouissance*. Ethical analysis opens the subject to *jouissance*, and thereby attempts to *defer*, interminably, the arrival of an ideal self.

Encore

> All that is not One must ever
> Suffer with the wound of Absence
> And whoever in Love's city
> Enters, finds but room for One
> And but in One-ness, Union.[9]

When the question of the relation of psychoanalysis and ethics comes up again in *Seminar XX, Encore*, Lacan treats it as inescapably related to the question of woman, or more precisely, to Freud's infamous question, *Was will das Weib?*, *What does the woman want?* As it turns out, Lacan's remark that nothing can be said about "the woman" in question in Freud's question has proven to be equally infamous. "*The* woman" in question "does not exist," Lacan says, and in order to designate this, he captitalizes the first letter of the definite article and writes the article crossed through: "*The* woman can only be written with *The* crossed through," he says; "There is no such thing as *The* woman" (1975, 68). By saying that "*The* woman" does not exist, however, Lacan does not imply "an ontology, or, what comes down to the same thing, a system" (66), and although it has been seized upon as such and as affirming a masculine position of mastery, his statement does not refer to this or that woman, to women in general, or to the essence-nature of the female sex. At issue in Lacan's statement, rather, is the manner in which historical representations of woman are bound up with narcissistic idealizations. Situated in the same beyond of language as is the Good in traditional ethics, "the opaque place of the *jouissance* of the Other" (77), "*The* woman" exists only as a fantasy, an imaginary idealization. Lacan says in *Encore* that this fantasy of "*The* woman" enables the male to assume the phallic position ("when one is a man, one sees in one's partner what serves oneself, what serves as one's narcissistic support" [80]). At the same time, the image-fantasy splits the woman ("she, the woman is differentiated from it," from the image, from "*The* woman" [79]). What the idealization comes down to, then, is that "love is impossible" (81), or at least that as long as love (*amour*) is soulful love (*âmour*), there is no nonbinary relation between the sexes: "as long as soul souls for soul [*l'âme âme l'âme*], there is no sex in the affair" (78).

The mystic texts that Lacan recommends reading in *Encore* seem to bear this out. Mysticism is a discourse of love. Its autobiographical narratives tell of a lover's progress toward a state of union with an Other, a state arrived at *via* the path (*la voie*), the so-called Mystic Way.[10] Often, in the tradition of the biblical *Song of Songs*, these are told as stories of spiritual marriage, where the divine is portrayed as a Bridegroom and the mystic is portrayed as a bride. Lacan's mystics—St. Teresa of Avila, Bernard of Clairvaux, Hadewijch d'Anvers, John of the Cross—use this spiritual marriage motif. The nuptial imagery requires that the mystic's soul be represented as woman whether the mystic writer be male or female. Thus in Hadewijch d'Anvers' (293–96) Epiphany vision, her soul appears as a festively attired bride who is led by an eagle to the embrace of her waiting Bridegroom. John of the Cross writes of the "delightful surrender" of his soul in the bed of her Beloved "in which the bride tastes much more steadily the delights of her Bridegroom" (501). And Bernard of Clairvaux says of his soul that "she has been gifted not merely with great knowledge of him who is her Bridegroom and God, but with his friendship and familiar intercourse. She has enjoyed his frequent colloquys and kisses, and with a daring born of this intimacy can say to him, 'Tell me where you pasture your flock, where you make it lie down at noon' " (189).

Given that the goal of this amorous relationship is the consummated union of Bridegroom and bride, mystic texts distinguish betrothal from marriage. The former, Teresa tells us, while requiring mutual agreement, implies that "the two persons are frequently separated" and that each "remain[s] a thing in itself" whereas in spiritual marriage, "the soul remains all the time in that centre with its God" (1989, 214). In the actual marriage, the soul is "conformed to God, in one Being and in one work" (Hadewijch 1980, 296). The nuptial union, then, accomplishes an *identification* of the Bridegroom and bride so that, as John of the Cross puts it, "even though neither changes their being, both appear to be God" (497). A *correlation* takes place in which, John says, "the two become one, as we would say of the window united with the ray of sunlight, or of the coal with the fire, or of the starlight with the light of the sun" (512). Teresa of Avila describes the marital union this way:

> it is like rain falling from the heavens into a river or a spring; there is nothing but water there and it is impossible to divide or separate the water belonging to the river from that which fell from the heavens. Or it is as if a tiny streamlet enters the sea, from which it will find no way of separating itself, or as if in a room there were two large windows through which the light streamed in: it enters in different places but it all becomes one. (1989, 214)

This notion of the identification of the two lovers elevates the feminine soul into the beyond of language, into the place of God. To use Lacan's terminology from *Seminar XX*, the soul becomes "*The* woman," situated in the place of the Other. Not to be confused with the female mystic or with this or that individual woman, *The* woman "does not exist" save as the mystic writer's imaginary idealization. This is not to say, however, that *The* woman has nothing to do with the female sex. "This Other," Lacan says, "while it may be one alone, must have some bearing on what appears of the other sex" (1975, 65). For in order that the bridal soul occupy the place of the Other, she must be differentiated from woman-in-the-flesh. Hence the essential virgin/whore typology as a major mystic marriage motif: it represents woman as divided, and it divides the woman from the man. Bernard preaches, for example, that the virgin soul is "beautiful among women," that is among "people who are sensual and worldly, people devoid of manliness . . . people who are entirely superficial, soft, and effeminate . . . people who, unlike herself, are not spiritual" (189–91). John of the Cross writes that in the virgin soul, appetites and passions are dried up and subdued "which in our flesh are the breasts and milk of mother Eve, and an impediment to this state [of spiritual marriage] . . . in which the soul kisses God without contempt or disturbance from anyone. For in this state neither the flesh, the world, the devil, nor the appetites molest her" (499). John explains the phrase, "girls of Judea," on the other hand, as having reference to the soul's "lower parts," because as he puts it, "girls attract lovers to themselves by their affection and grace" just as "sensory operations and movements" of the soul "strive persistently to attract the will of the rational part to themselves . . . to draw it out of its interior to a desire for the exterior things which they crave . . . to move and attract the intellect that it may be wed to them in their base way of feeling" (484).

So too Teresa: her writing is no less reliant on the man/woman and woman/woman binaries than is that of Bernard or John. In one of her poems, for example, she plays on the Spanish *velar* ("watch") and *velo* ("veil") by way of enjoining the nuns of Carmel to "manfully" guard the virgin-veil, "And let no thief your house assail," lest the Bridegroom close the nuptial door, "And you will never see Him more." For Teresa, to take the "comely" virgin veil is to stand guard over the maiden-veil, lest the bride become that other woman: "On sentry duty you must stand"; "With ready-lighted lamp in hand, / Veilèd, your vigil you must keep / And look you never fall asleep, / But with your loins well-girded stand"; "Live steadfastly and keep your vows. / Then you will enter with your Spouse / All glorious in your nuptial veil, / *So you must watch and never fail*" (1946, 304–5). If spiritual marriage is to be consummated, Teresa insists, the other woman, the soul's *fleshly body*, must die. In one instance, resorting to Christianity's familiar conflation of female sexuality and hunger, she compares the soul before the marital union to a silkworm "which is fat and ugly," but which "then dies, and a little white butterfly, which is very pretty, comes forth from the cocoon" (1980, 342). If they are to become brides of Christ, Teresa tells her sister nuns, they must suffer abnegation of their fleshly ("fat and ugly") selves: "Therefore, courage, my daughters! Let's be quick to do this work and weave this little cocoon. . . . Let it die; let this silkworm die" (343). "Oh daughters," she sighs in her *Meditations on the Song of Songs*, "if you knew what great evil lies enclosed here. The body grows fat and the soul weakens" (1980, 228).[11]

Luce Irigaray, like Stephen Heath, is critical of *Encore* and of its appeal to Bernini's *Ecstasy of Saint Teresa*, for reproducing the scene of the phallus. Irigaray argues that the splitting of woman is accomplished by and for men as "a prop for their souls-fantasies" (1985, 96), and that where the woman Teresa is concerned, "her own writings are perhaps more telling" (91). What Teresa's writings seem to tell, however, is that female mystics are themselves caught up in the idealization/abjection of woman, that, to use Lacan's words, "women too are soulful lovers, that is to say that they soul for the soul" ["*les femmes aussi sont âmoureuses, c'est-à-dire qu'elles âment l'âme*"] (1975, 79). Both male and female mystics engage in a representation through which, as Jacqueline Rose puts it, "woman is constructed as an absolute category (excluded and elevated at one and the same time)," a representation which locates unity "on the side of the man" (1982, 47). That this splitting of woman makes violence to the female body a condition of the mystic's dream of homologisation suggests how important representation is for structuring "the sexual relation." Lacan emphasizes this. But he also says that the fantasy of oneness, the misrecognition at the root of representation, is a cover-up which cannot succeed. "When Lacan is reproached with phallocentrism at the level of his theory, what is most often missed is that the subject's entry into the symbolic order is equally an exposure of the value of the phallus itself," Rose maintains. "The subject has to recognise that there is desire, or lack in the place of the Other, that there is no ultimate certainty or truth, and that the status of the phallus is a fraud (this is, for Lacan, the meaning of castration)" (40). "*The* woman" *wants*: the dream of unity inevitably fails.

In *Encore*, Lacan says that "there must be a *jouissance* that exists beyond [*qui soit au-delà*]. That is what one calls a mystic" (1975, 70). I turn now to some concluding remarks on the manner in which this *jouissance* works in the mystic text as an enactment of the failure of unity. In the end, perhaps, it is for their staging of this failure that Lacan refers to these texts as "the best things you can read." What they dramatize, ultimately, is not so much a specular "soulmorality" as the ethical turn toward alterity that Lacan speaks of in *Seminar VII* ("*Avez-vous agi conformément au désir qui vous habite?*"), and again in *Seminar XX*, when he says that "to speak of love is in itself a *jouissance*" (77).

En-corps

If you think you have understood, you are bound to be wrong.

Lacan, *Freud's Papers On Technique*

It is the function of psychoanalysis, we might say, to have the subject discover that its place is not the place of unity or certainty, the place of (the desire of) the Other, but "somewhere else." Freud sought the place of the subject in the field of the dream—not, Lacan points out, because the dream is the "somewhere else" of the subject, but because it is the royal road to it (1977a, 258). Lacan notes that Freud was "interested only in the elaboration of the dream," that is in "what we would now call its linguistic structure" (259). What actually interests Freud, Lacan says, "is the message as interrupted . . . discourse" (1988b, 125). For it is in interruption, rupture, that the "somewhere else," the unconscious of the subject, breaks in upon the dream-text. To speak of the unconscious as the place of the subject is not to speak of a localizable or representable place, then, but of a disruption, a discontinuity, "which takes the place of representation" (1977b, 60), and which displaces the referential subject.

Thus when Lacan says in *Seminar XI* (20) that, given intervening developments in structural linguistics, the field of the unconscious is "more accessible" to him than it was to Freud, the point is that what linguistics affords Lacan is not access to a particular place, but a way of understanding the unconscious as the *dis-place* of the subject. And as is suggested by his inversion of Saussure's formulation of the sign, which elevated the signified over the signifier and so returned language to representation, Lacan takes the signifier to be primary to the development of this understanding of the unconscious. The signifer/signified formula implies "that the signifier has an active function in determining certain effects in which the signifiable appears as submitting to its mark," Lacan says (1977a, 284). The formula implies that the signified submits to the signifier, rather than the other way around, and therefore that language functions not so much to represent as "to signify *something quite other than what it says*" (155). The inversion of Saussure's formula of the sign thus suggests the "over-turning" (*renverser*), the change of direction, mentioned above. It is not the case, for Lacan any more than for Lyotard, that a pre-existent subject uses language to convey meaning, to represent. Rather, according to Lacan, language, through the differential paths (*les voies*) of the signifier, is constitutive of the subject-as-displaced. The unconscious "speaks," *stages* its "presence," through the differential *play* of the signifier, such that a text, rather than representing a unified subject's certain truth, performs a dramatic presentation of what Lacan calls "the self's radical ex-centricity to itself" (171).

"At the heart of the subject is a certain *punctuation*," Weber suggests. The subject "can never in and of itself constitute 'an object of cognition,' since it consists in the interruption and suspension of beings, rather than in their codification" (Weber 1991, 97). Lacan's own language, his texts, can be understood as enacting this punctuation: "what his texts give voice to and in a certain sense 'stage' is not simply something represented, an object that would be self-identical" but "a mode of articulation which might best be described as a 'slip-up' or derailing of sense: the language of the unconscious, the unconscious as language" (1). The text as comic drama: "a 'fundamental failure' of action in order to return to the desire which resides there, a ceaseless fading of the object, a scorn for knowledge, an ambiguity of meaning in witty words, mutual misunderstandings among the characters on the stage. Lacan the actor pulls out all the gimmicks through which a theory of desire unfolds" (de Certeau 1986, 51). This theatricality extends beyond the scene of Lacan's seminars to his psychoanalytic career, punctuated as it is by discontinuities, displacements, deferrals: the life, like the text, a trope, not to be taken "seriously," or at least, not to be taken as offering truth.

We would be mistaken to expect truth from the mystics either, from their dream-texts of spiritual marriage, from these, "the best things you can read." For rather than closing their narratives on the soul's arrival at union, the mystics tell us that as soon as the soul feels the touch of her Bridegroom "[j]ust as quickly, she feels His absence and the impossibility of possessing Him here as she wants" (John of the Cross 1964, 423). The mystic texts "punctuate the Lacanian space where they figure as *exordia* (where does it begin?) or as exits (where to end?)," de Certeau says (1986, 59). These texts, too, enact the failure of the unity ideal. The bridal soul, always "hoping for what it lacks" (John of the Cross 1964, 421–22), yet finding "no rest or relief" (421), remains "in constant suffering at the absence of her Beloved" (424). I am suggesting that what is acted out, for Lacan, on the stage of the Cornaro chapel, is this performance of the unconscious itself, "the unconscious, not as an object of perception or of intuition, not as a clinical object, but as a theatrical scene" (Weber 1991, 11).

Such a drama must be played out in a language that unsettles meaning. Hence, the mystic's recourse to the allegory of spiritual marriage, to allusions, apostrophes, equivocations, exclamations, quotations, interrogations, puns, and other outbursts of "sweet disorder" (Teresa of Avila 1989, 10), to language that "let[s] something of their experience overflow in figures and similes . . . rather than rational explanations" (John of the Cross 1964, 408). The mystic texts, in which the narrating "I" keeps falling off meaning, cannot pretend to mastery, to the posturing of a unified self. While Teresa is commanded by her confessors to write, and while she submits herself carefully to their judgement and use, "for I am under an obligation not to dispute with my superiors, but to obey them, and it would not be right for me to dispute with them" (1989, 67), the Teresa who writes and who likens the self to a multifaceted, multimansioned crystal-castle ("we ourselves are the castle" [31]), cannot stop "talking nonsense" (31), "wandering from the point" (64), "dreaming" (1957, 99), and in general, "becoming unwrought" (103). As Jacqueline Rose points out, the narrating subject is split from the opening "I" of Teresa's *Meditations*, which quickly shifts to "you," then "we," refusing to be pinned down, enacting "a precariousness in language which reveals that neither the subject nor God can be placed ('speaking with one person, asking for peace from another, and then speaking to the person in whose presence she is')" (Rose 1982, 52).

Similarly, the mystic's puns, such as Teresa's sliding of *velar* into *velo*, enact a destabilizing of the subject and of meaning. And although apparently intended to banish the flesh, the puns and the tropes *re-turn* signification to the heterogeneous body, figuring alterity back into the text. Spirit slides into sense when John explains that for a soul indisposed, "the fire usually holds back without entering the wood," while "in the prepared soul, the act of love enters immediately" (593); or when he says that "severe dryness" in love is unpleasant, "not gentle, but afflictive," while wetness is "delightful" (586). More than just semantic shifting, this slide from the lofty heights of an ethereal Other to a body that knows desire "even in the outermost joints of the hands and feet" (603), gives primacy to the material signifier. The mystic texts, remarkable for the manner in which their figures work through "an *interplay* of sound" (Howe 1988, 167, my italics), invite what Garrett Stewart (1990) calls a "phonemic reading," where the text as signified yields place to, is displaced by, the drama of signifiying. Such is de Certeau's reading of John's *Spiritual Canticle*. The long poem, de Certeau (1986, 99) says:

> abounds in rich rhyme patterns, internal assonance and phonic repetitions, all within a structure transferring the words, pronouns, and verbs of the one (*thee*) to the other (*me*): a music of echoes and minor images in which the *Amado* is doubled, bursts, and retrieves himself in the gaze and advent of the other—but which other? Saussure's anagram rule and Ruwet's rule of parallelism—both of which establish the primacy of the signifier over the signified—here seem to be confirmed by the

play of nouns ('wound,' 'quest,' etc.), which shift freely from
one position to the other, thus destroying the stability of the
characters to whom they are attached.

What is it to write or to read? The mystic, as writer, "utters a thousand
follies" (Teresa of Avila 1946, 97–98). The mystic writer can do no more
than stammer, says John of the Cross: "Stammering, a trait we notice in
children's speech, means that one is unsuccessful in saying and explaining
what one has to say" (John of the Cross 1946, 440). John's long poem, the
Canticle, never stops stammering, "deconstructing meaning and making it
music. . . . It says nothing. It permits saying" (de Certeau 1986, 99). As
such, as stammering, mystic writing is what Lacan calls "serious" (1975,
70). It shows us that the drama of sameness and difference is played on the
level of fantasy—and that the fantasy is perfectly "deconstructible" ("*un
fantasme parfaitement désarticulable*" [81]). We might even want to say that
it "deconstructs itself." *What do we do when we do analysis? What is it to write
or to read?* What is important for Lacan in either case is to give status to the
unsayable, to *something unrepresentable* that yet contaminates representation with spoils and spots. We can call this something the unconscious, as
long as we are careful to note that in naming it, we have not said where or
what the unconscious is. "Hence, the drama in the true sense of the word,
of his quest," Lacan says of Freud. "The drama which, in each of the cases
he gives us, ends in failure." If Freud opened up the path (*la voie*) of the
signifier as the path to the unconscious, as the way to the "promised land,"
one cannot say "that he entered into it;" one cannot say that he ever
arrived (1988a, 15).

In accompanying Freud to the "promised land," Lacan, we might
say, failed as well. No subject is the receiver of the "Love Letter" he sends
in *Le Séminaire XX*. No ethics arrives with *Encore*. Perhaps the status of
his seminar "is ethical," however, because as a dramatization of the unconscious, it does not present its self as norm. "Clearly the unconscious
suggests that there is in the speaking something, somewhere, which
knows more than he does, but this something cannot be represented as a
model for the world," Lacan says (81), leaving the "something more" of
Encore in the realm of "perpetual ambiguity" (81).

4

L'Écriture limite

DISCOURSE OF A CRISIS IN IDENTITY

person (O.E.D.): a mask used by a player, a character or personage acted (*dramatis persona*), one who plays or performs any part; in the general philosophical sense: a self-conscious or rational being

The mirror no longer exists in which a monolithic logos—a "monologic"—once appeared. . . . [T]his passing beyond representation, this work which destroys it, has always been the "other" of theological discourse, has always constituted theatrical space, in which the "I" puts on the mask of equivocal laughter or sexual excesses in order to mime the drama of his analysis, that is, of his death. From the Greek Menippean satire on to Lucan and Petronius, to the medieval carnival—a theatre with no stage and therefore with no audience and no performance, for everyone involved is his own author and actor, his ego and his alter ego—to Rabelais and Swift, to Joyce, Artaud and Bataille, the deathly laughter of this deconsecrated "I" becomes stronger and clearer, more biting and effective. It destroys the monologic of representational literary discourse and sets the general scene for a kaleidoscopic and pluralist way of writing in which we see nothing, for it is the writing which sees us.

Kristeva, "The Ruin of a Poetics"

Here I use "person" to identify those entities that are self-conscious, rational, and self-determining. Such a use of "person" is important, for it will help to determine which entities exist that can act as we, that can know they exist and act, and which can, then, reflect upon their knowledge and action and take responsibility for it. This use of person arises in discussions of the existence of other minds and can be construed as an epistemological use of the term. The exploration of such epistemological issues (e.g. on what grounds can I know that an entity is a person?) requires rendering the definition of person as a concept as precisely as possible. Such precision will be an ontological quest to be clear about a category of reality. . . . One should note that interest in defining the concept of person is not just ontological or epistemological. One is not simply concerned with categorizing the entities that furniture the world. One is interested as well in the concept of person due to its role in ethical theory. Thus, in addition, one will be interested in identifying those entities that are self-conscious, rational, and self-determining, because they will, as well, be the moral agents of the universe.

H. Tristram Engelhardt

A Depressive Moment: Everything is Dying

Julia Kristeva says in *Black Sun* that in times of crisis or loss, *melancholia* asserts itself, "establishes its archaeology, generates its representations" (8). Her essay, "Holbein's Dead Christ" (1989a, 106–38), concerns one

87

of melancholia's representations, Hans Holbein the Younger's *The Body of the Dead Christ in the Tomb*, generated at a time of upheaval and religious crisis in Europe. The date of the painting, 1522, places it on the threshold of the modern and at the point where the Aristotelian-Christian cosmology is in the process of collapsing. The painting depicts the newly dead body of Christ laid out on the slab of a tomb. The corpse is painted life-size and as seen from the side, its chest, hands and feet bearing the marks of torture, and its head slightly turned toward the viewer to reveal that "the expression of a hopeless grief; the empty stare, the sharp-lined profile, the dull blue-green complexion are those of a man who is truly dead, of Christ forsaken by the Father ('My God, my God, why have you deserted me?') and without the promise of Resurrection" (110). That the painting is only twelve inches high, portraying the tomb as narrow and closed and with a low ceiling which bears down on the corpse, "intensifies the feeling of permanent death: this corpse shall never rise again" (110). Even the sheet which covers the slab on which the corpse is stretched out, signifies the irrevocability of this death: "[t]he very pall, limited to a minimum of folds, emphasizes, through that economy of motion, the feeling of stiffness and stone-felt cold" (110).

Kristeva opens her essay by quoting Prince Myshkin in Dostoyevsky's *The Idiot* who, on seeing a reproduction of the Holbein painting at Rogozhin's house, exclaims, "Why, some people may *lose their faith* by looking at that picture" (107). Kristeva herself reads the painting as conveying such loss of faith. Holbein's is a disenchanted vision, she says; his dead Christ, walled-in by black stone, is utterly without transcendence, "without any prospect toward heaven . . . distant, but without a beyond" (113). She suggests that the painter's vision of a desacralized world generates his minimalist aesthetic: the pall, reduced to a minimum of folds, "the well-nigh anatomical stripping of the corpse" so as to render death unadorned (110). Holbein "isolated, pruned, condensed, reduced" (115) his work into a "chromatic and compositional asceticism" (123). Representing a world devoid of transcendence, "the artist refused to cast an embellishing gaze" (127).

And just as the artist's minimalist aesthetic suggests to Kristeva the new vision of reality being born in Europe at the time, "[a]nother, a new morality resides in this painting" (113). Holbein "leaves the corpse strangely alone" (112), she writes, its isolation heralding the detachment of the newly emerging individual, now "autonomous," left to rely on its self. The modern moral subject, betraying "[n]o exalted loftiness toward the beyond" is "strangely lonesome. Self confident. And close" (138). Moreover, this subject, cut off from heaven, has put the excesses of the body away. Hence, the new morality, like the Holbein painting, will be a study in stone-cold langauge. It is as if, with the death of Christianity's God, comes the death of medievalism's desiring (erotic and paroxystic) body. This is Kristeva's suggestion in "The Bounded Text" (1980a, 36–63). Once "the transcendental unity" supporting the medieval symbol, "its otherworldly casing, its transmuting focus," gave way and Western culture moved into the "ideologeme of the sign," she says, the body was reduced and *reified*, turned into an *object* "in the strongest sense of the word" (39–40). At the same time, the body was valorized, "transformed into an *objectivity*—the reigning law of discourse in the civilization of the sign" (40).[1]

"The Bounded Text," which first appeared in *Sémeiótiké* (1969), precedes the psychoanalytic perspective that had come to inform Kristeva's work by the time she wrote "Holbein's Dead Christ." In the latter essay, the transition from medieval to modern is said to constitute a traumatic loss of the Other, a severance of the pole of desire which linked the medieval subject to God. No longer available to Holbein is the medieval sacrificial economy—portrayed by Lacan's mystics as a spiritual marriage—through which death is "destroyed and superseded" (1989a, 131) by being cast as an experience of becoming *homologous* with the divine.[2] And with this loss of (the desire of) the divine Other, Kristeva says, goes an entire ascetic and martyrizing tradition which "magnified the victimized aspect" of the sacrifice of the body "by eroticizing both pain and suffering, physical as well as mental, as much as possible" (131). Thus in the Holbein painting, there is "[n]ot a single impulse that betrays *jouissance*" (138). With the transcendent pole of desire cut, the body is no longer representable, through sacrificial death, as *aufgehoben*, and the eroticism of pain is now lacking. The modern text "identifies not with desire but with *severance*" (137), Kristeva writes. With melancholia as the symptom of its loss, the new discourse treads "the tightrope—as the represented body—of an economical, sparing, graphic rendition of pain . . . a serene disenchanted sadness . . . a mastery of harmony and measure" (136).

At the conclusion of "Holbein's Dead Christ," Kristeva asks whether it is "still possible to paint when the bonds that tie us to body and meaning are severed?" (136). Is is still possible to paint, or to write, *after* the death of the body? Kristeva's work can be read as an attempt to respond to this question, the question of the possibility of a practice of signification, or to use her more theatrical term, of *signifiance*, which does not retreat into the solace of religion and so reconnect the subject's bond to the divine Other, but which does not function either as a modern metalinguistic or monological system in which "the subject both assumes and submits to the rule of 1 (God)" ("Word, Dialogue, and Novel," in 1980a, 77). A monological system is "centered on an *entity* Descartes called a *subject*," who is "not included, dissolved, or implicated in the system" but rather "hovers above it, subdues it, and is absent from it," she says (1984d, 94). Although "a fixed point" and "the sole guarantee of the symbolic system and its logical laws," the monological subject "calls himself 'we'" and in so doing presupposes that his or her addressee "is made in the image of its 'we'—an indifferent subject, supposedly everyone, since symbolic systematicity eliminated heterogeneity by eliminating the negative and unfolds, purporting to be transparent, eternally communicable, omnivalent" (95). Because the addressee is not included in this system save as a mimetic reflection of its addressor-subject, the monological subject/object model of signification is, for Kristeva, as closed or hemmed in (*suturé*), as Holbein's harrowing tomb, as unfolded as his minimalist pall. Kristeva writes so as to re-fold the text. She seeks modes of *signifiance* that respect the heterogeneity of the addressee.

For her, then, to paint or to write *after* is not a matter of reproducing the "new morality" announced by Holbein's *Dead Christ*—although it is, inescapably, a question of what she calls the *ethical function* of the text (1984d, 232). She distinguishes her notion of the ethical "from the 'scientific morality' that would like to found a normative, albeit apparently libertarian, ethics based on knowledge" (234). As is the case for Lacan, "ethics," for Kristeva, is not a moralism grounded in a monological subject, a prescriptivism that "preaches the foreclosure of the subject-as-model" (234). The question of ethics, and thus of writing *after*, cannot be asked apart from "a perspective that takes account of the process/trial of the subject in language or, more generally, in meaning" (233), she says. Based in part on her autobiographical essay, "My Memory's Hyperbole," what follows here is an outline of Kristeva's theory of *le sujet en procès*, the subject-in-process/on trial, as it develops in her writing from 1965 to 1974, and as it relates to what she takes to be the ethical function of the text. I turn then to her well-known essay, "Stabat Mater," as a practice-performance of the "ethical." I conclude this chapter by attempting to relate Kristeva's psychoanalytic ethics to "feminism" and "postmodernism."

s'exiler: to go into exile; to expatriate one self

> *L'exil coupe les liens, et jusqu'aux plus profonds, ceux*
> *du Sens, ceux qui nous attachent à la croyance que*
> *ça—la vie—a Un Sens, garanti par un père mort.*
> Kristeva, "Un nouveau type d'intellectuel:
> le dissident"

In 1984, Kristeva wrote the essay, "My Memory's Hyperbole," for inclusion in an anthology of female autobiographies edited by Domna Stanton and titled *The Female Autograph*. Stanton explains in her preface (vii–viii) that she excised *bio* from *autobiography* in the volume's title in order to bracket the traditional emphasis on autobiography as the recounting of "a life," with "that notion's facile presumption of referentiality," and to suggest that the women's writing in this collection does not so much narrate as "*graph* the *auto*." Kristeva's essay, written in the first person plural, a form which she adopts in place of the objective and authorial "I," and offered as *hyperbole*, not to be taken literally, is in keeping with this nonreferential understanding of the self. "My Memory's Hyperbole" traces through the evolution of the so-called *Tel Quel* group in Paris, from the time of Kristeva's arrival late in 1965 until 1974, when she published her *Revolution In Poetic Language*. The essay does provide a scheme, then, an outline of intellectual and political developments, but written as the auto(bio)graphy of a "we" that remains hyperbolic. As Stanton (x) describes it, Kristeva's essay "confounds generic and generic boundaries" as it discusses intellectual and political movements in Paris, "analyzing the various scenes, acts, and dramatis personae not merely as a critical observer, but undeniably as a major protagonist." The essay is written as a dramatization of *its self*, of the ongoing production-mutation of a hyperbolic "subject-in-the-making" (1981b, 167), a subject which, Kristeva says, "is alive only if it is never the same" (1984c, 220).

Kristeva writes as a *dramatis persona*, a player in the drama, "a revolutionary actor, a 'scriptor' of events" (Caws 1973, 3), rather than as the detached and stable person-subject that has dominated moral philosophy since Locke's *Second Treatise*. Thus her writings must be dissociated from the idea of the text as object or propertied product, authored and controlled by the person-subject, and aligned instead with performance or practice, "the practice of scription," for which the text as "the visible 'stage' (in the theatrical sense), cannot be envisaged within the myth of representation (mimesis): it is a 'performance,' a 'production,' actively involving writer and reader alike; it needs to be conceived as a materiality rather than an outer form enclosing an inner content" (Roudiez 1974, 297). The text, conceived as such, as what gives identity, *graphs the auto*, "a kind of matrix that makes its subject" (1984a, 131), is also constitutive of *soma*. "[S]igns are what produce a body," Kristeva says (132), again dissociating her understanding of the subject as *dramatis persona* from the person of private rights, whose assumption of ownership and control of his or her propertied body, places the reified body "before" and "outside" the object-text.[3] The practice of the text as scription "brings to our own critical practice and textual theory something that is unmistakably alien," Leon Roudiez suggests ("Introduction" 1980a, 11). It made of Kristeva, on her arrival in Paris, what Roland Barthes called *l'étrangère*, not just a "foreigner" from Bulgaria,[4] and not just an outsider to the standard theoretical scene, but a scriptor whose writing, "the discourse of a crisis in identity" (1984c, 268), exiles the unified subject.[5]

Kristeva says in her preface to *Desire in Language* (ix) that such writing "assumes the necessity of adopting a stance involving otherness, distance, even limitation" as "the only guarantee of ethics" in a world of technological rationality. Her early essays, many of which are published in *Séméiotiké* (1969), attempt to move literary criticism and structuralist linguistics from the monological, or "zero-one," system to this ethical stance involving otherness, to the "zero-two" practice of "poetic language." Kristeva applies the latter term to writing which is open to the subject's production as both an "I" and an other. In Bakhtin's approach to poetic language, for instance, where "[t]he word/discourse is, as it were, distributed over the various instances of discourse that a multiple 'I' can occupy simultaneously," the subject of language "is made up of otherself," becomes in writing its "own otherness, and thereby multiple and elusive, polyphonic" (Kristeva 1973, 109). According to Bakhtin's understanding of the carnivalesque, "all poetic language is dramatization, dramatic permutation . . . of words," Kristeva says; what it dramatizes is the scene of the subject, in process between representation and rhythm: "On the omnified stage of the carnival, language parodies and relativizes itself, repudiating its role in representation; in so doing, it provokes laughter but remains incapable of detaching itself from representation" (Word, Dialogue and Novel," in 1980a, 79). In that this dialogical, "zero-two," poetics is simultaneously one and the other, "both representative and antirepresentative" (79), it allows for what she calls an "ambivalent ethics" (69): never simply a rational monologism, and "[p]ut together as an exploration of the body" (83).

In "Pour une sémiologie des paragrammes," (in *Séméiotiké*) Kristeva uses Ferdinand de Saussure's *Anagrammes* to develop the notion of a paragrammatical text, the text as an interrelation of texts, a multifaceted juncture of meanings and codes.[6] Like Bakhtin's dialogical "word," the poetic paragram is always at least double, and therefore ambivalent (1969, 182–83). In this same poetic "doubling" of the subject and language, Kristeva identifies what she calls the "ethical dimension" of Roman Jakobson's work ("The Ethics of Linguistics," in 1980a, 26–35). Jakobson's reading of the futurist poets is an "opening" of monological theory to the "*other* of the linguistic and/or social contract" (30), which thereby enables the speaking subject "to shift the limits of its enclosure" (33). By giving voice to the rhythm inscribed in Mayakovsky's poetry, Kristeva says, Jakobson allows us to hear the "silent causality and ethics" (28) at work in poetic language.[7] Again, ambivalence allows for ethics: for Jakobson, language is double, both rhythm and structure, both struggle and law; and therefore the writing subject is never either monological reason or asymbolic rhythm, but an unending dialogical, ethical process-production between the two.

These early essays suggest that the ethics of a given discourse "may be gauged in proportion to the poetry that it presupposes" (25); and that the function of ethical writing is to "dynamize" structure through a theory-pratice of the text as "a free play, forever without closure" ("From One Identity to an Other," in 1980a, 128). An ethics based on this zero-two writing emphasizes "the dynamics of production over the actual product" and therefore the *otherness* (*alterité*) of what it studies, rather than focusing on a reified and representable object (1969, 39–40). And since the text is inseparable from subjectivity, shifting toward the other of poetic language implies a similar spatialization of the writing subject, and suggests the need for a theory of this subject as itself a productive activity in language. In that it opens to the space (matrix, field, network) of the subject, Bakhtin's dialogism is, for Kristeva, "quasi-psychological" (1973, 110), and a precursor of this needed theory of the subject. She says the same of Saussure's research on poetic language, published in his *Anagrammes*. Studying Saturnian verse and Vedic poetry, Saussure discovered that each message was a double code: "each text was another text, each poetic unit had at least a double signification, no doubt unconscious, that was reconstituted through the play of the signifier"

(Kristeva 1989b, 293). What he had isolated was the seemingly psycho-analytic particularity of poetic functioning: "that supplementary meanings slip into the verbal message, tear its opaque cloth, and rearrange another signifying scene" (293).

Kristeva's psychoanalytic theory of the subject *en procès* receives its first systematic elaboration in *Revolution in Poetic Language* (1974). Here, in an attempt "to go beyond the theatre of linguistic representations to make room for pre- or translinguistic modalities of psychic inscription" (1987a, 5), she borrows the term *chora* from Plato's *Timaeus* and uses it to designate both *anteriority* and *heterogeneity*. The *chora* signifies a mythical space or phase "anterior" to the mirror stage and the child's acquisition of language, a preverbal "rhythmic space, which has no thesis and no position" (26). It also designates a heterogeneousness beyond representation, an unconscious supplementarity which, although unrepresentable, belongs inescapably to the process of *signifiance*. From the *chora* emanate the energy charges which Kristeva associates with the operation of the "semiotic" (*le sémiotique*). As "articulated by flow and marks: facilitation, energy transfers, the cutting up of the corporeal and social continuum as well as that of signifying material" (40), the semiotic is distinct from the "symbolic" (*le symbolique*), language as representation, meaning, sign. Always "ambivalent," signification requires both the semiotic and symbolic modalities. Even as the metalanguage of a monological subject, signification cannot completely close off the semiotic, and neither is there any possibility of meaningful signification outside the pro-positioning of a conscious subject. The psychoanalytic *sujet en procès* is interminably in-process/on-trial between the semiotic and symbolic.

Related to this distinction of the semiotic and symbolic is Kristeva's theory of the text as a production, "a process, an *engendrement*" (Lewis 1974, 30) which includes both *géno-texte* and *phéno-texte*. She uses the latter term "to denote language that serves to communicate." The phenotext, she says, is a structure which "obeys rules of communication and presupposes a subject of enunciation and an addressee" (1984d, 87). The genotext, however, is not a linguistic structure but a generative process, "a *process*, which tends to articulate structures that are ephemeral (unstable, threatened by drive charges, 'quanta' rather than 'marks') and nonsignifying (devices that do not have a double articulation)" (86), but which are nonetheless detectable in the phenotext. Although, as Christopher Johnson points out, "[t]he relationship linking the geno- and pheno-texts is one of translation" (1988, 74), Kristeva does not think of "translation" as the "zero-one" passage from an underlying original to a surface copy. There is, she says, no one-to-one correspondence between the genotext and the phenotext, such as is suggested by Chomsky's Cartesian model of deep structure and surface structure. For Kristeva, the genotext is not an *other scene* but an *ensemble of other scenes*. Thus it is generative of signifying operations which exceed the limit of sentence-meaning ("L'Engendrement de la formule," in 1969, 281–84). Through these signifying operations, the genotext imprints its seal in the phenotext, leaves markers (such as the phonemic-phonetic elements or groups of elements which Kristeva calls *signifying differentials*) which open "the normative usage of language on the one hand toward the underlying and repressed body and semiotic *chora*, and on the other hand toward multiple displacements and condensations which produce a *strongly ambivalent* if not *polymorphous semantics*" (1974, 34).

This practice of the text as scription, as both genotext and phenotext, therefore as "more-than-a-sentence, more-than-meaning, more-than-significance ... always *more*: more-than-syntactic" ("The Novel as Polylogue," in 1980a, 168), is coextensive with what Kristeva calls ethics.[8] "The ethical cannot be stated," she says in *Revolution in Poetic Language*; "instead it is practiced to the point of loss, and the text is one of the most accomplished examples of such a practice" (234). A textual practice is ethical when it is ambivalent: "positing and dissolving meaning and the unity of the subject therefore encompasses the ethical" (233). One cannot demand, then, that the text simply "emit a message which would be considered 'positive': the univocal enunciation of such a message would itself represent a suppression of the ethical function as we understand it" (233). Only when it *both* posits *and* "pluralizes, pulverizes, 'musicates'" (233) meaning does the text fulfill its ethical function. There is no authoritative position for a unified person-subject above or outside of this text. Kristeva's subject is an exile, a wanderer (*égaré*), a subject whose only place, locus, is language and thus whose position (identity, meaning) can never be fixed (see 1977a).

"reaching out to the other, the ethical"

No language can sing unless it confronts the Phallic Mother. For all that it must not leave her untouched, outside, opposite, against the law, the absolute esoteric

> *code. Rather, it must swallow her, eat her, dissolve*
> *her, set her up like a boundary of the process where "I"*
> *with "she"—"the other," "the mother" becomes lost.*
>   Kristeva, "The Novel as Polylogue"

Perhaps no essay of Kristeva's has garnered more critical attention, especially from feminists, than "Stabat Mater." First published in *Tel Quel* (1977) as "Héretique de l'amour," the essay appears in *Histoires d'amour* (1983), and in English translation in *Tales of Love* (it is also printed in English in *Poetics Today* 6, 1–2 [1985] and in *The Kristeva Reader*). Kristeva explains that the title of the essay is taken from the mournful hymn of the Roman Catholic Church, "Stabat Mater Dolorosa," attributed to the medieval poet Jacopone da Todi, a meditation on the Virgin Mary in her station at the cross which opens with the words, "The sorrowful mother was standing." Kristeva refers to the composer Pergolesi, "who was dying of tuberculosis when he wrote his immortal *Stabat Mater*" ("Stabat Mater" in 1987b, 252). Might the hymn, then, and Kristeva's essay along with it, be two more of melancholia's representations? For melancholy, which points to a loss, a crisis, can be traced to the subject's being "irrevocably, desperately separated from the mother," Kristeva says in *Black Sun*; "a loss that causes him to try to find her again, along with other objects of love, first in the imagination, then in words" (6). Pergolesi, the composer, at the critical moment of his dying, turns in his *Stabat Mater* to a paradigmatic representation of maternal love: Mary, defying her son's death, *the masculine corpse*, through love, prompts the outburst, "'*Eia Mater, fons amoris!*' ('Hail mother, source of love!')" (252). Pergolesi returns to the lost mother, "the primal shelter that insured the survival of the newborn," and so "overcomes the unthinkable of death by postulating maternal love in its place—in the place and stead of death and thought" (252). And Kristeva recalls the same "lost territory" (234), the primal mother, in her "Stabat Mater," where she takes as her subject Christianity's fantasy of Mary, "doubtless the most refined symbolic construct" (234) through which primary narcissism has been idealized.

The idealization involves less the representation of an archaic mother than "the idealization of the *relationship* that binds us to her," Kristeva contends (234). She takes this relationship as the actual "subject" of her "Stabat Mater," not however, simply to talk about "it," to reify primary narcissism as the object of a theoretical discourse, but to enact the idealization's "analysis" (division, dissolution) of the writing subject. The essay,

I am suggesting, can be read as a staging of Christianity's narcissistic drama. As such, Kristeva's writing in the essay oscillates between the symbolic representation of primary narcissism, and the semiotic processes that are supplementary to the idealization and that expose it for the fantasy it is. In writing the essay, Kristeva says, she wanted to position her self this way, to dramatize the process/trial between the semiotic and symbolic, "to give an image of this contradiction which is on the one hand a description of the universal and the individual, and on the other hand, the involvement of the author" (1984b, 24). Kristeva "wanted to give an impression of a sort of wound, a scar" (24).

The essay, then, is not coherent. It cannot be read as a zero-one. It is both a "theoretical or academic discourse . . . a knowing discourse, a discourse which pretends to some objectivity," and simultaneously, "a sort of literary poetic text" (24). While the theoretical discourse, the analysis-overview of the historical cult of Mary, dominates the main text which is placed on the right side of the essay, theory is by no means confined there, but surfaces also in the bold-face inserts which interrupt the main text and are printed on the left side of the essay. Thus the typographic fragmentation of the essay does not mark a clear division between the "theoretical" and the "literary" (can such a separation ever be made?). Even less does the right side correspond to the rational and paternal symbolic, while "[t]he left-hand column, heavily inked and broken into short sections, lyrically invokes the pre-cultural maternal body" (Jones 1985, 95). The essay does not simply bifurcate along the line of a left/right, semiotic/symbolic, before/after, female/male binary, as several of Kristeva's critics maintain. To read the essay this way—to say, for instance, that Kristeva identifies the semiotic with "femininity," placed "outside" (to the side of) the patriarchal symbolic, and that "Stabat Mater" thus proclaims a biological essentialism (a conservative apology for motherhood, an exclusion of women from the realm of power)—is to miss the ambivalence of Kristeva's signifiying subject, its undecidable process between semiotic and symbolic, which is also the undecidability of a (sexual) identity.[9] Both the right and the left sides of the essay are *always both* semiotic and symbolic, both representation and something unrepresentable.

Hence the ambivalence of the semiotic *chora* in "Stabat Mater": it is "readable" on both sides of the essay and on the levels of both signified and signifier. The *chora* is "readable" both as representation, as an idealization of primary narcissism, and as unrepresentable unconscious operations which work within representation to disturb its coherence. *As an idealization* of the relationship to the primal mother, the *chora* represents the dreamed recovery of an intra-uterine, neo-natal bond with the mother ("recovered childhood, dreamed peace restored" (1987b, 247), whose sheltering love focuses adoringly on the sleeping (male) child, his "forehead, eyebrows, nostrils, cheeks, parted features of the mouth, delicate, hard, pointed chin. Without fold or shadow, neither being nor unborn, neither present nor absent, but real, real inaccessible innocence, engaging weight and seraphic lightness" (247–48). This idealization of primary narcissism is assimilated by Christianity's Mary, whose virginity, immaculate conception, and assumption into heaven as Queen, gather together "the attributes of the desired woman and of the holy mother" (245) to produce an "incredible construct" (256) of maternal love, centered on the son, beholden to the husband and father (243). To the consternation of several of her critics, Kristeva *represents the fantasy* of primary narcissism by folding autobiographical reflections on her own role as phallic mother, reminiscences drawn both from her mothering and from her practice as an analyst, into the historical myth. This is not an exercise in re-membering intended to promote a return to the primeval mother. It is, rather, a procedure of *anamnesis* (240), such as we have seen described by Lyotard: a technique of working through (up and down, back and forth, between the two columns) Western culture's representation of woman to the heterogeneity that representation "forgets."

To expose primary narcissism as a fantasy is to introduce a division which is incongruent with the supposed unity of the originary mother-child bond, a "continuous separation," an "abyss between the mother and the child" (254) that precedes both biology and memory. The division is already there in the subject of signification, which means that the mythical "territory" is "lost" because it does not, and cannot, exist. For the subject in language, there is no safe place or space, no "extra-symbolic" haven, before or outside the law, Kristeva says.[10] Thus the semiotic *chora* is ultimately neither representable nor localizable. It is "knowable" only as an *after-effect* of the genotext, a remainder, a "heterogeneity that cannot be subsumed in the signifier" and that fractures the narcissistic myth, "extract[ing] woman out of her oneness" (259). Intonation and rhythm are two markers of this semiotic heterogeneity in "Stabat Mater." For instance, both columns juxtapose regular sentences with unpunctuated fragments, as well as with sentences "punctuated" so as introduce semantic and syntactical anomalies: abrupt halts or musicating ambiguities.

Intonation and rhythm work as well through repetition of phonemes and networks of alliteration (*signifying differentials*) which, to use Kristeva's words, "establish trans-sentence paths that are superimposed over the linear sequences of clauses and introduce into the logical-syntactical memory of the text a phonic-instinctual memory. They set up associative chains that crisscross the text from beginning to end" ("The Novel as Polylogue," in 1980a, 169), and we might say, from column to column: the procedure of anamnesis, a *passing through* and beyond the sign, spatializes the textual network. Where intonation and rhythm work by means of the falling/failing of pronouns (the shifting and ambiguous "I": Kristeva's voice inseparable from Mary's voice, the maternal voice from the voice of infancy, the voice/identity of the poet from that of academic), signification is destabilized, as is the identity of both sender and receiver.

In all of these cases, the intonational breakthrough is a going through to the "polylogical body" ("The Novel As Polylogue," in 1980a, 186). This is not a phonocentric endeavor, for given that the mark which the genotext leaves in the phenotext is an "illegible *seal*" that has to be read ("L'Engendrement de la formule," in 1969, 285), "[t]he eye cannot be excluded by the ear" ("The Novel as Polylogue," in 1980a, 180) from detecting the heterogeneity in language. For instance, Kristeva's play on the word "perversion" in "Stabat Mater" (260) must be seen in order to be "heard" as a *distortion* of the *verse au père*. Procreation (the mother's pregnancy, childbirth), as jubilatory "outpouring," is "feminine perversion" as *père-version*, she says, as a culturally coded buttress of the father's law and of the repression of woman-as-body, of the body of woman. Contrary to this paternal law, to the father's "proper" name, and distorting of his image in the mirror, "Stabat Mater" practices another kind of perversion: it allows the semiotic *chora*, figure of the perverse, to insinuate itself into the essay. It is this contamination of primary narcissism by the unconscious that makes "Stabat Mater" an incestuous text. It is a "strange incest" ("The Novel As Polylogue," in 1980a, 192), however, where what is being swallowed is an idealization: the phallic mother, destructured-dissolved by traces of the unconscious which are enfolded in the surface text.

A "strange fold" ("Stabat Mater," in 1987b, 259), too. The uncanniness of "Stabat Mater" is not the *Unheimliche*, the phobic affect, *abject*, the terrified loathing associated with the body of the pregnant woman and reproduced by feminists who recoil from the essay because they read it as appealing to this woman.[11] For the body which grafts itself as other within this essay cannot be represented. It is the encounter with this unrepresentable other, this unsaid, Kristeva suggests, which produces the feeling of uncanny strangeness. The *Unheimliche* "is a *destructuration of the self*" which results from "a new encounter with an unexpected outside element"; it is "a crumbling of conscious defenses, resulting from the conflicts the self experiences with an other—the 'strange'—with whom it maintains a conflictual bond" (1991, 188). The unconscious, the *unheimlish* place, at once alien and immanent within representation, "our disturbing otherness . . . that threat, that apprehension generated by the projective apparition of the other at the heart of what we persist in maintaining as a proper, solid 'us'" (192), puts "Stabat Mater" into what Lyotard calls an economy of deferral. Disposed to go counter to what is proper, to turn the wrong way, change direction, go awry, the essay weaves together both symbolic and semiotic, and so fails to fix an either/or identity for its self.

"What can be our place in the symbolic contract?"

> *Ethics used to be a coercive, customary manner of ensuring the cohesiveness of a particular group through the repetition of a code—a more or less accepted apologue. Now, however, the issue of ethics crops up wherever a code (mores, social contract) must be shattered in order to give way to the free play of negativity, need, desire, pleasure, and* jouissance, *before being put together again, although temporarily and with full knowledge of what is involved.*
>
> Kristeva, "The Ethics of Linguistics"

In "Women's Time," Kristeva relates her understanding of ethics to three types, or what she calls three "generations," of feminisms. The first of these types, she says, constitutes an avoidance of the problematic of the (father's) law. This is feminism-as-romanticism ("a kind of naive romanticism" [1981a, 138]). It aspires to a foreign land outside patriarchal society, "an a-topia, a place outside the law" (1981c, 27). For such feminists, belief in an essential female identity goes hand in hand with the utopian dream of a distinct place for women, a countersociety based on the qualitative difference of women from men, and "imagined as harmonious, without prohibitions, free and fulfilling" (27).[12] This dream of a separatist *space* is also the dream of a female *time* outside the linear temporality of patriarchal history (the dream, for instance, of re-membering the cyclical body/time of the pre-patriarchal primeval goddess). A second generation of feminisms, Kristeva says, constitutes not an avoidance of, but a capitulation to, the law. This is feminism as a "logic of identification" (19) with the ontology and morality of the patriarchal system, with its conscious subject and his proprietary rights. This type of feminism strives to gain for women a space in linear time. It claims equality for women as full partakers of the social contract, as *persons* "reducible one to the other" (20), but in so doing, Kristeva says, it assumes that contract's binary model of (sexual) difference.[13]

There is, however, a "third generation" of feminists, Kristeva maintains, feminists who advocate neither the identification with power nor the constitution of a fetishist counterpower, feminists for whom "the sociosymbolic contract as a sacrificial contract" (25) has become a major concern. Recognizing that no signification, no meaningful communication, is possible without separation and positing of differences, these feminists, she says, do not promote rejection of the patriarchal symbolic in favor of a harmonious before or outside. But neither do they accept modernity's order of identity and difference as an ontological given. "[W]ithout refusing or sidestepping" the logic of separation and syntactical sequence on which language and the social contract are founded, these feminists attempt "to explore the constitution and functioning of the contract" and in particular "to break the code, to shatter language, to find a specific discourse closer to the body and emotions, to the unnameable repressed by the social contract" (24–25).[14]

The contract is sacrifical: for Kristeva, there is no escaping this. Rather than being an accord among equals (equal men) as modernity advertised it, the social contract, she says, is based "on an essentially sacrifical relationship of separation and articulation of differences" (23). Kristeva applies the term "religion" to any symbolic system that orders the violence of such a sacrificial relationship, "binds it, tames it" (29). In this view, religious systems are what facilitate the violent separation of sameness from difference and are constitutive of subjectivity and the social contract: "I call 'religion' this phantasmic necessity on the part of speaking beings to provide themselves with a *representation* (animal, female, male, parental, etc.) in place of what constitutes them as such, in other words, symbolization—the double articulation and syntactic sequence of language, as well as its preconditions or substitutes (thoughts, affects, etc.)" (32). Both separationist and conformist feminists would thus have with some affinity with what Kristeva calls "religion." At the same time, through her analysis of feminism in its "third generation," Kristeva situates the women's movement "within the very framework of the religious crisis of our civilization" (32). Rituals and representations of sacrifice, such as the myth of the primal mother, no longer serve to satisfy the fear and anguish associated with symbolic violence, she says. And herein lies the importance of third generation feminists, where "the word 'generation' implies less a chronology than a *signifying space*" (33).[15] What third generation writers attempt to explore is the ambivalent space of the signifying bond itself, she maintains, the "interior" space of "*the founding separation of the sociosymbolic contract*" (34), where meaning and subjectivity are constructed. This work of the third generation replaces the "attempt to fabricate a scapegoat victim as foundress of a society or a countersociety . . . by the analysis of the potentialities of *victim/executioner* which characterize each identity, each subject, each sex" (34).

Such work, for Kristeva, is ethical. It undertakes its task in order to emphasize *responsibility*, the responsibility which each of us has to put "fluidity into play against the threats of death which are unavoidable whenever an inside and an outside, a self and an other, one group and an other, are constituted" (35). But although ethical, such work is a *perversion*, a contamination, of the dominant morality. The question of "postmodernism," for Kristeva, and she does pose postmodernism as a question, as a question of writing or signifying *after*, is the inquiry, the exploration, of the ethical, so understood. Like the term generation, "postmodernism" for her, implies not a chronology but a signifying space, a spatializing of signification: it "attempts to *expand the limits of the signifiable*" (1980b, 137). Its concern "extends deep within the constituent mechanisms of human experience as an experience of meaning; it extends as far as the very obscure and primary narcissism wherein the subject constitutes itself in order to oppose itself to another" (137–38). At this level of sacrificial interiorization, at the threshold where subjectivity is constructed through the demarcation and separation of an other, the "borderline writing" (139) of postmodernism attempts to shift the boundaries, the limits, of the subject's enclosure.

For Kristeva, there is melancholy implied in this "writing-as-experience-of-limits" (139), undertaken in a time of crisis and, as she puts it, "in such an unprotected manner" (141), that is, without the refuge of religious representations, and so without the defense of an idealized life-giving mother. But the melancholy of the "postmodern ethical" is not, for her, the miserable sadness that Holbein sees in the silent, stone-cold cadaver of Christ. It is not the melancholy that results from the modern subject's reification and repression of the body as dead, and as a threat to be abjected. "The corpse, seen without God and outside of science, is the utmost of abjection," Kristeva says in *Powers of Horror* (4). But in "postmodern" (poetic, psychoanalytic, feminist, aesthetic) practices, the body comes back to life. For the heterogeneity of the "postmodern text," she says, is the heterogeneity of the signifying body, released ("resurrected"?) from its murderous Cartesian enclosure. If, however, "postmodern" practices bring the body to life, they do so by putting the unified subject to death: the unified self perishes (L *cadaver*, f. *cado*, *cadere*, to fall, fall down, fall dead, decay, perish; a dead man's remains), "literally 'falls into pieces' " (1989a, 18)[16] in what Kristeva calls the "text."

Not either life or death then, but an ambivalence between the two. As representation, *l'écriture limite* is caught up necessarily in symbolic violence and the threat of death. But as the interminable upheaval/crisis of the signifying subject, it opens to death's unrepresentability: the unrepresentable as index of the death drive, "the ultimate imprint of the death drive," working as the "nonrepresentative spacing of representation" and so as the dissolution of the transcendental self (1989a, 27). Etymologically, Kristeva points out, analysis means *dissolution*: to unbind, dissolve, cut, divide, dislocate, lose.[17] Psychoanalysis does not liberate us into self-completion and wholeness, she says. Its "ethical" task, instead, is to record, to dramatize, the *crisis* of the unified self. Ethical analysis works as unceasing deferral, " 'that's not it' and 'that's still not it'," because it reaches out to "something that cannot be represented, something that is not said, something above and beyond nomenclatures and ideologies" (1981a, 137).

PART THREE

5

Comings and Goings

FOUCAULT'S CATACHRESIS

A plethora of intelligibilities, a deficit of necessities.
Foucault, "Questions of Method"

Before he died in 1933, the French poet, novelist and dramatist Raymond Roussel committed to a publisher a short monograph which was printed posthumously as *How I Wrote Certain of My Books*. It was understood that the text, which by its title promises to reveal the process by which Roussel worked, would not be published during his lifetime, Michel Foucault notes in *Death and the Labyrinth: The World of Raymond Roussel*: as if only Roussel's death could reveal what is hidden within what the writer himself called his "secret and posthumous" book; and as if the death, a suicide on the threshold of a closed door, would be the key which unlocked the secret of Roussel's enigmatic body of work (1986, 4–5). It may be, however, as Foucault suggests, that Roussel's death itself was a ritual part of the secret of his life's work, a secret kept secret until his death, and intensified and made definitive by the revelation, in death, that *How I Wrote Certain of My Books* "hides as much, if not more, than it promises to reveal" (5). For Roussel's book, which purports to be an autobiographical narrative, provides only "fragments of a breakdown of memory" (5), Foucault says. These fragments, moreover, are presented so as to subvert the chronological order of the narrative form. They foreground the process which Roussel used to compose his early writings, but barely outline the mechanisms employed in the intermediate novels, *Impressions d'Afrique* and *Locus Solus*, while the

107

more recent plays *La Poussière de Soleils* and *L'Étoile au Front* "are mere specks" which receive almost no attention, and the late work, *Nouvelles Impressions* "can be identified only by what it is not" (2). By means of this folding of the point of revelation into a distant background, Foucault says, Roussel's text:

> reverses the triangle of time. By a complete revolution, the near becomes distant, as if only in the outer windings of the labyrinth Roussel can play the guide. He leaves off just as the path approaches the center where he himself stands, holding all the threads at their point of entanglement or—who knows?—their greatest simplicity. (2)

One might be tempted to read this comment on Roussel's enigmatic autobiography as itself an autobiographical remark, particularly given the interview published at the end of *Death and the Labyrinth* (169–86) in which Foucault, while offering an account of his writing of the book on Roussel, suggests a marked affinity between Roussel's style and his own. Foucault was, he says, "quite young"—he gives the year as 1957, the place as the *librarie* José Corti, "that huge bookstore across from the Luxembourg Gardens," the occasion as his return from Sweden to France for the summer, even a description of the bookseller in question and a record of the conversation between them—when he chanced upon Roussel's *La Vue* and was, from the first line, "completely taken by the beauty of the style" (171). In reading *La Vue*, Foucault recounts, he experienced a "shock of recognition." There was something about Roussel's writing style that "immediately absorbed" him: "I was taken by the prose style even before learning what was behind it. . . . Slowly and systematically I began to buy all of his works. I developed an affection for his work, which remained secret, since I didn't discuss it" (172–73). The secret of Foucault's affection remained secret at least until 1963, when he published *Death and the Labyrinth*, his analysis of the "lovely curiosity" (175) that is Roussel's style.

Or, perhaps the secret remained so longer, even up to the time of Foucault's death in the middle of a proposed six-volume series on the history of sexuality and sexual ethics. This is the suggestion I consider in the present chapter, where I take issue with an interpretation of Foucault's work that is offered by Hayden White in "Foucault's Discourse: The Historiography of Anti-Humanism" and Simon During in *Foucault and Literature: Towards A Genealogy of Writing*. As different as these two sources are—White's study is entirely dismissive, for instance, while During's is highly nuanced and sympathetic—both make similar claims that I wish to question. The first of these concerns the reading of Foucault's work, particularly the "catachretic" style of writing that he takes from Roussel and that he employs in his analysis of power, as fundamentally nihilistic, as an operation bent on disclosing the "structure of deception and duplicity" (White 1987, 113) on which all social formations, including discursive systems, are based. I will argue that what Foucault's work attempts to uncover is not meaninglessness but multiplicity; that his intention is to read social texts as plural and folded, and thereby, to facilitate responsible change. The second claim concerns a so-called aesthetic turn (During 1992, 12) in Foucault's later thought. The claim here is that a break occurs between Foucault's early work, including *Death and the Labyrinth*, where he is said to be interested in avant-garde literature, linguistic tropes, and the question of style as a question of *transgressive writing*, and his later works, including the *History of Sexuality* series, where he is said to conceive of style as a (previously hidden) *transgressive self-fashioning*, an autobiographical aesthetics of life. While I will explore "autobiographical" connections between the Rousselian style that Foucault studies in *Death and the Labyrinth* and the style of his *History of Sexuality* series, particularly *Volume One*, I will not look to these texts as narrating or exhorting a conduct of life. The *History of Sexuality* series is not Foucault's way of disclosing a personal secret, a transgressive (sexual) stylistics of life that, in White's words, he "wanted to hide yet allowed to appear" (1987, 21); and it is not to Foucault's "manner of living" (During 1992, 12) that we ought to look for a conjunction between ethics and stylistics in his later work. I will argue that this interpretation not only repeats a conventional separation of textuality and ethics, reducing the latter to a normative conduct, a life-style or code of existence; but also that it misses the real ethical significance of Foucault's work. I submit that we should look for a link between ethics and aesthetics in Foucault not in an auto-*bio*-graphical revelation of his life-style, but in his signature practice of the text.[1]

Eventalization

The mono-logical vocabulary of repression pervades *The History of Sexuality*'s opening pages, where Foucault announces the hypothesis which, in this introduction to a proposed six-volume analysis of the history of sexuality, he will attempt to call into question. The *repressive hypothesis* is first of all a thought of the essence, he says, the essence of the single entity, "sex," which, from the early seventeenth century and on into the "monotonous" Victorian regime, could no longer safely be named. The repressive hypothesis has it that until the dawn of the seventeenth century, "a certain frankness was still common, it would seem," and the body and its passsions had not yet been confined: "It was a time of direct gestures, shameless discourse, and open transgressions, when anatomies were shown and intermingled at will, and knowing children hung about amid the laughter of adults: it was a period when bodies 'made a display of themselves' " (1990, 3). But this openness supposedly gave way to the modern prohibiton which confined "it" to a single locus, the parental bedroom, and to one heterosexual, procreative norm. As well as being a thought of the essence, Foucault maintains, the repressive hypothesis is also a history of "sex," which, "after hundreds of years of open spaces and free expression" (5), became an infamous object of secrecy that could be talked about only under strict conditions and according to rule that separated licit from illict, either silencing the latter, or confining it within the brothel, the mental hospital, or other such "places of tolerance" (4). The historical narrative, in turn, presents a theory of power. The repressive hypothesis understands power to be monolithic, a mechanism of prohibition or censorship imposed on "sex" from without. And, in that this account makes the prohibition coincide with the development of capitalism, the "minor chronicle of sex and its trials is transposed into the ceremonious history of the modes of production" (5), Foucault says, so that the story of the subjugation of sex is made part of a grand narrative of capitalist exploitation. A theory of sex, a theory of history and of the history of sex, a theory of power and of the relation between power and sex, the discourse of repression is, finally, a discourse of emancipation, a discourse through which sex "becomes legitimately associated with the honor of a political cause," that is, through which sex, or "the sexual cause—the demand for sexual freedom," is "placed on the agenda for the future" (6). It is the political agenda, Foucault suggests, that confers "the speaker's benefit" on the proponent of the repressive hypothesis: "If sex is repressed, that is, condemned to prohibition, nonexistence, and silence, then the mere fact that one is speaking about it has the appearance of a deliberate transgression." Simply to hold forth in the language of repression is to place oneself "to a certain extent outside the reach of power" (6).

In *The History of Sexuality*, Foucault asks not why we are repressed, but why we say we are repressed; why, in a society such as ours, "where the devices of power are so numerous, its rituals so visible, and its instruments ultimately so reliable, in this society that has been more imaginative, probably, than any other in creating devious and supple mechanisms of power," we hold onto the theory of repression, this "negative and emaciated form of prohibition" (86). For Foucault, to explore the question will be to trace the spirals by which we came to affirm that sex is negated, and by which we were led "to show, ostentatiously, that sex is something we hide" (9). The spirals themselves will prove to be channels of power, discrete paths that power takes "within a general economy of discourses on sex in modern societies since the seventeenth century" (11). Foucault takes it as his task in *The History of Sexuality* to locate some of these myriad channels, and so to analyze power relations as *open* strategies through which historical experiences of sexuality took shape. This task is quite distinct from that of countering the repressive hypothesis with another (repressive) discourse of truth, "a discourse in which sex, the revelation of truth, the overturning of global laws, the proclamation of a new day to come, and the promise of a certain felicity are linked together" (7). Foucault himself never resorts to a repressive hypothesis. As he put it in a 1978 interview, "I never use the word power with a capital P" (1989a, 185). Rather, he attempts through his analyses to demonstrate "the heterogeneity of power," how power "is always born of something other than itself" (186), how then it permits of change. For Foucault, the question of power is always at the same time the question of change, or as he put in the same interview, power:

> is only one aspect of the problem which I wanted to confront; the other is the one of resistance. If mine were an ontological conception of power, there would be, on one side, Power with a capital P, a kind of lunar occurrence, extra-terrestrial; and on the other side, the resistance of the unhappy ones who are obliged to bow before power. I believe an analysis of this kind to be completely false, because power is born out of a plurality of relationships which are grafted onto something else, born from something else, and permit the development of something else. (187)

Yet it is precisely as a propounding a metaphysics of Power that Hayden White reads *The History of Sexuality*. In the book, he says, power is "hypostatized and given the status that spirit once enjoyed in an earlier, humanistic dispensation" (1987, 134). It is the purpose of all of Foucault's writing to expose the hidden operations of power in discourse, White maintains. In Foucault's earlier writings, this exposé targets the distinction between signifier and signified, between an order of words and an order of things, the very distinction on which discourse itself depends, yet a distinction which Foucault takes to be "as false as it is insidious" (112). According to Foucault, White says, we should not seek "some correlation of 'what is said' with an 'order of things' that preexists and sanctions one 'order of words' as against another" (111), for the rules that determine different discursive formations, that govern what in a given time and place can and cannot be said, are rules in service to power, not to truth or signification. White cites as examples *Madness and Civilization*, *The Birth of the Clinic*, and *The Order of Things*, books on psychiatry, medicine, and the human sciences, in which, he says, Foucault attempts to demonstrate that such distinctions as those between madness and sanity, sickness and health, and truth and error are products of social controls exercised during particular periods, rather than products of knowledge resulting from hypothesis and observation. In short, to close "the gap opened up by the distinction between 'words and things' " (113), the early Foucault "undertakes to expose the dark underside of discourse" (113), to disclose the gap as a void, an absence at the heart of language, which is also the space where power resides. Foucault's work "looks like history, like philosophy, like criticism, but it stands over against these discourses as ironic antithesis," White writes. "It even assumes a position superior to that of Foucault's own heroes, for Foucault's 'discourse about discourses' seeks to effect the dissolution of Discourse itself. That is why I call it catachretic" (115).[2]

In traditional rhetorical theory, White points out, the term catachresis (L abuse; G misapplication, misuse [of a word]) presupposes the distinction between the literal and figurative meanings of words, or more generally, between "proper" and "improper" usage. But in the case of Foucault, for whom, White says, "all words have their origin in a 'tropological space' " (115), for whom "the distinction between literal and figurative meaning goes by the board—except as an indication of the power of discourse to constitute 'literality' " (115)—all discourse is catachretic. All language "constitutes an abuse" (116). White argues that up to the sexuality series, catachresis enjoys a privileged place in Foucault's work, not only because it suggests the fundamental deception that underlies discourse, but also because it furnishes Foucault with a theory of tropes (metaphor, metonymy, synecdoche, irony) through which to characterize the *épistème* of a given age.[3] Through the latter use of catachresis, Foucault has at least a theory "that might be used as a staging area for some 'positive' conception of 'knowledge' "(130). But with *The History of Sexuality*, White maintains, Foucault gives up on his tropological analysis of different modes of discourse, for now "[e]verything is seen to consist in 'power' " (130). Now, discourse is conceived to be so saturated with power "that it is no longer distinguishable from it" (130). Now, White says, Foucault, always "close to the nihilism of Nietzsche" (105), becomes a thoroughly negative and apocalyptic thinker: "And the whole of culture, far from being that exercise of endless sublimation that humanism conceives to be the essence of our humanity, is revealed as nothing but repression. More or less killing, to be sure, but in the end nothing but destructive" (134).

I propose a different reading, beginning with those pages of *The Order of Things* (110–15) where Foucault considers what he calls the "tropological space" of language, the space of meaning's original deferral. At one time, Foucault speculates, "everything had a name—a proper or peculiar name. Then the name became attached to a single element of the thing, and became applicable to all the other individual things that also contained that element: it is no longer a particular oak that is called *tree*, but anything that includes at least a trunk and branches" (1970, 113). In this displacement of words from their original meaning through the multiplication of figures or tropes, "language developed and gradually drifted away from primary designations" (113). Foucault would even suggest that "words were figurative before being proper: in other words, they had scarcely attained their status as particular names before they were being scattered over representations by the force of spontaneous rhetoric" (114). In any case, his point is that "words have their *locus* not in *time*, but in a *space* in which they are able to find their original site, change their positions, turn back upon themselves, and slowly unfold a whole developing curve" (114). The slipping mobility has always been there and it belongs not simply to "figurative" language, but "to all language whenever it is spontaneous" (114).

In the earlier *Death and the Labyrinth*, the tropological space of language serves as the point of departure for Foucault's analysis of the work of Roussel. Here, as in *The Order of Things*, the mobility of words stems from their sparsity, from "the simple, fundamental fact of language, that there are fewer terms of designation than there are things to designate"

(1986, 14). This sparsity, Foucault says, is itself "a two-sided experience," for the deficiency of words is at the same time a source of "remarkable richness;" the tenuousness of language that which dispatches it in at least "two different directions" at once (14). From *lack* stems a prodigious *fecundity*, and the twisting, forward-and-backward, looping of language within what Foucault calls Roussel's "tropological space." Roussel's writing:

> demonstrates the duality of language which starts from a simple core, divides itself in two, and produces new figures. (It's a pro-liferation of distance, a void created in the wake of the double, a labyrinthe extension of corridors which seem similar and yet are different.) In their wealth of poverty words always refer away from and lead back to themselves; they are lost and found again; they fix a vanishing point on the horizon by repeated division, and then return to the starting point in a perfect curve(14–15)

This "marvelous property of language" (1986, 15) is, at least in part, behind what Foucault, in *The History of Sexuality*, refers to as the "veri-table discursive explosion" that takes place around sex during the so-called age of repression. Rather than presenting us with a single discourse on sex, he says, the seventeenth to nineteenth centuries generated a steady proliferation of discourses concerned with sex, "a discursive fer-ment that gathered momentum from the eighteenth century onward" (1990, 18). The single word, "sexuality," cannot account for the wealth of "sexualities" produced by this discursive ferment which, in the inter-ests of silencing sex, became an incitement to speak endlessly about it. Foucault suggests that in the sphere of the Catholic sacrament of pen-ance, for example, although discretion was advised as to the naming of sexual acts, the scope of the examination of conscience continually increased so as to attribute more and more importance to myriad insinua-tions of the flesh: "thoughts, desires, voluptuous imaginings, delecta-tions, combined movements of the body and the soul; henceforth all this had to enter, in detail, into the process of confession and guidance" (19). The penitential discourse, which insists on pursuing "down to their slen-derest ramifications" (19) all the stirrings of the desire in the confessing self, thus "had to trace the meeting line of the body and the soul, follow-ing all its meanderings" (20).

From the early to the late modern periods, then, "we are dealing less with *a* discourse on sex than with a multiplicity of discourses" (33), and with a multiplicity for which heterogeneity, not uniformity, is the rule. It would be a mistake, Foucault says, "to see in this proliferation of discourses merely a quantitative phenomenon, something like a pure increase" through which legal sanctions are intensified and repressive controls are more strictly enforced (36). For the discourses which proliferate are different one from another, emanate from different sources, and operate in different institutional sites. Through their proliferation, uniformity is "broken apart, scattered, and multiplied in an explosion of distinct discursivities which [take] form in demography, biology, medicine, psychiatry, psychology, ethics, pedagogy, and political criticism" (33). In this process, the entity, "sex," is spread across a multiplicity of heterogeneous centers, and beyond the reach of the sought-for containment. A double progression: the policing of sex through its insertion into discourses of management and utility is a restriction that multiplies, a containment that explodes, such that intensification of power links to a multiplication of discourses and to a dispersal across a network of variable sites. "So it is not simply in terms of a continual extension that we must speak of this discursive growth; it should be seen rather as a dispersion of centers from which discourses emanated, a diversification of their forms, and the complex deployment of the network connecting them" (34).

What is opened up by this polymorphous dispersion, rather than the truth or secret of sex, is what Foucault in the Roussel book calls "a space of infinite uncertainty" (1986, 9), a space in which the sex that is "driven out of hiding and constrained to lead a discursive existence" (1990, 33) continues to escape control: "It may well be that we talk about sex more than anything else; we set our minds to the task; we convince ourselves that we have never said enough on the subject, that, through inertia or submissiveness, we conceal from ourselves the blinding evidence, and that what is essential always eludes us, so that we must always start out once again in search of it" (33). Unhiding is hiding, as in the evolving confessional, where that which, above all else, has to be confessed, is always presented "as the disquieting enigma: not a thing which stubbornly shows itself, but one which always hides, the insidious presence that speaks in a voice so muted and often disguised that one risks remaining deaf to it" (35). In other deployments, for instance nineteenth-century genetics and reproductive counseling, where the aim of the discourse seems to be "not to state the truth but to prevent its very emergence," Foucault suggests that "a refusal concerning the very thing that was brought to light and whose formulation was urgently solicited" (55), is what masks, or bars access to, "the unhidden." In Charcot's Salpêtrière, Foucault says, it is misunderstanding (*méconnaissance*) which, at the last moment, masks the truth which an enormous apparatus for observation has been set up to disclose (56).[4] His point is that the proliferating discourses which constitute sex as a problem of truth are themselves, and for diverse reasons, a heterogeneous weave of misunderstandings, avoidances and evasions, which hide at least as much as they reveal.

What *The History of Sexuality* inevitably places in question through these introductory analyses of the modern Western discourse of sex as what might be called a tropological space—a network of overlapping heterogeneities within which meanings multiply and spiral off in different directions at once—is the assumption of a detached, spectating subject, what Foucault in *The Order of Things* (xiv) calls the "phenomenological" pose. For instance, Foucault considers the centrifugal movement toward the heterosexual couple as being, at the same time, a scrutinizing elaboration of all manner of peripheral sexualities, so that sex "came apart" rather than coalescing into unity, and so that "[t]he area covered by the Sixth Commandment began to fragment" (1990, 39). Among other things, this surplus at the border "opens up a universe without perspective," to use Foucault's words from *Death and the Labyrinth*: "There is no privileged point around which the landscape will be organized and with distance vanish little by little; rather, there's a whole series of small spatial cells of similar dimensions placed right next to each other without consideration of reciprocal proportion" (1986, 107). Nor is there discoverable, within the field of proliferating peripheral sexualities, the subject/object, inside/outside binary that the spectating subject requires. Thus, in the case of children's sex, one of those forbidden areas ostensibly sentenced to nonexistence under the repressive regime, no binary division can be drawn between the inside and the outside, between verbosity and silence. The stifling of the sexuality of children was not a simple imposition of silence, Foucault says:

> Not any less was said about it; on the contrary. But things were said in a different way; it was different people who said them, from different points of view, and in order to obtain different results. Silence itself—the things one declines to say, or is forbidden to name, the discretion that is required between differ-

ent speakers—is less the absolute limit of discourse, the other side from which it is separated by a strict boundary, than an element that functions alongside the things said, with them and in relation to them within over-all strategies. (1990, 27).

That for Foucault, the inside, as Gilles Deleuze (1986, 98) puts it, is "merely the fold of the outside," and that the self is constituted "as an always other or a Non-self" through this same process of folding, is a theme which, Deleuze notes, Foucault analyzes in depth in the book on Roussel: "For what Raymond Roussel had discovered was the phrase of the outside, its repetition in a second phrase, the minuscule difference between the two (the 'snag' [*l'arroc*]) and the twisting and doubling from one to the other. The snag is no longer the accident of the tissue but the new rule on the basis of which the external tissue is twisted, invaginated and doubled" (98). *Death and the Labyrinth* "presents in a literary and humorous way" what could be demonstrated by the "serious" disciplines of epistemology or linguistics, Deleuze says. In the book, Foucault "has knitted or sewn together all the meanings of the word *doublure,* in order to show how the inside was always the folding of a presupposed outside. And Roussel's last method, the proliferation of parentheses inside one another, multiplies the foldings within the sentence. This is why Foucault's book on Roussel is important, and no doubt the path it traces is itself double" (1986, 98–99). The folding by which "the inside will always be the doubling *of* the outside" (99), obviates the binary division "between what one says and what one does not say" (Foucault 1990, 27), so that silence, or rather silences, become "an integral part of the strategies that underlie and permeate discourses" (27).[5]

The same principle of folding is the presupposition of the "first rule" for the analysis of power that Foucault proposes in *The History of Sexuality,* the rule of immanence. The rule states that, since there is no exteriority between techniques of knowledge and strategies of power, historical analyses must begin "from what might be called 'local centers' of power-knowledge" (98). In *The History of Sexuality,* the Catholic confessional, "the relations that obtain between penitents and confessors, or the faithful and their directors of conscience" (98), would be one such local center. "Here, guided by the theme of the 'flesh' that must be mastered, different forms of discourse—self-examination, questionings, admissions, interpretations, interviews—were the vehicle of a kind of incessant back-and-forth movement of forms of subjugation and schemas of knowledge" (98). The rule of immanence is the starting point for the kind of analysis that Foucault refers to elsewhere as *eventalization*:

> What do I mean by this term? First of all, a breach of self-evidence. It means making visible a *singularity* at places where there is a temptation to invoke a historical constant, an immediate anthropological trait, or an obviousness that imposes itself uniformly on all. To show that things "weren't as necessary as all that"; it wasn't a matter of course that mad people came to be regarded as mentally ill; it wasn't self-evident that the only thing to be done with a criminal was to lock him up; it wasn't self-evident that the causes of illness were to be sought through the individual examination of bodies; and so on. A breach of self-evidence, of those self-evidences on which our knowledges, acquiescences, and practices rest. This is the first theoretico-political function of "eventalization." (1987, 104)

Foucault's eventalization is not a thought of the essence. It looks for power not as an absolute outside of discourse, a simple prohibition whose objective it is to constrain, but as immanent within spoken and written texts, as enfolded within a tissue constituted by power, knowledge, and pleasure. With modern power, "[w]e are dealing not nearly so much with a negative mechanism of exclusion as with the operation of a subtle network of discourses, special knowledges, pleasures and powers," he says. "At issue is not a movement bent on pushing rude sex back into some obscure and inaccessible region, but on the contrary, a process that spreads it over the surface of things and bodies, arouses it, draws it out and bids it speak, implants it in reality and enjoins it to tell the truth: an entire glittering sexual array, reflected in a myriad of discourses, the obstination of powers, and the interplay of knowledge and pleasure" (1990, 72).

The rule of immanence, or of "singularity," presupposes variability across the wide dispersion of centers. The rule is already in practice in *The History of Sexuality*, for example, in Foucault's insistence that we are not dealing with the same tactics in the eighteenth- and nineteenth-century prohibition of consanguine marriages as in the control of children's perversions. The former "attempted to reach its objective through an asymptotic decrease in the thing it condemned, whereas the control of infantile sexuality hoped to reach it through a simultaneous propagation of its own power and of the object on which it was brought

to bear" (41–42). In the campaign moblized around the sexual pleasures
of children, the simultaneous back-and-forth propagation of power and
knowledge entailed the constituting of children's pleasures "as secrets
(that is, forcing them into hiding so as to make possible their discovery)"
(42). This in turn necessitated the construction of an entire medico-
sexual regime for which the "vices" in question were not such much the
enemy as the support. From devices of surveillance, to mechanisms for
compelling admissions, to diagnostic and corrective discourses, to the
recodification of pedagogy, the "sex" that was constituted as the evil to
be eliminated proliferated myriad means for its control. Hence power op-
erated in this local center not as a "barrier system," but as "indefinite *lines
of penetration*" disposed around the child. Always relying on the child's
"vice" as its support, "power advanced, multiplied its relays and its effects, while its target expanded, subdivided, and branched out, penetrat-
ing further into reality at the same pace" (42). In the process, pleasure
was not externalized to the outside of the power-knowledge network. On
the contrary, the network depended for its very propagation on "a physical proximity and an interplay of intense sensations" (44). Since the
medicalization of children's and other peripheral sexualities required that
the perversion in question had to be detected "in the depths of the organism or on the surface of the skin, or among all the signs of behavior,"
pleasure was doubled into the knowledge-power fold: "The power which
thus took charge of sexuality set about contacting bodies, caressing them
with its eyes, intensifying areas, electifying surfaces, dramatizing troubled
moments. It wrapped the sexual body in its embrace" (44). This sensual-
ization ensured that an impetus was given to power through its very exercise, that "the pleasure discovered fed back to the power that encircled
it," even as "power anchored the pleasure it uncovered" (44–45).

    In *The History of Sexuality*, Foucault suggests that his six-volume his-
torical analyses will follow this play of the back-and-forth—of the "pleasure that comes of exercising a power that questions" and of the "power
that lets itself be invaded by the pleasure it is pursuing"—this game of
capture and seduction, of attraction and evasion, "traced around bodies
and sexes, not boundaries to be crossed, but *perpetual spirals of power and
pleasure*" (45). And he suggests that he will analyse change, not by looking for who has the power in the order of sexuality and who is deprived of
it, and not by looking for who has the right to know and who must remain ignorant, but according to his "second rule" for the analysis of
power, the rule of continual variation, by charting continual modifica-

tions, constant shifts, across the network of local centers. Given the dissemination and flux that characterize this network of centers, Foucault says that his analyses of power will set out in two directions at once, as his "third rule," the rule of double conditioning suggests: it will be necessary to focus attention both on the matrix or field across which power is dispersed, and as well on the smallest sites or points which saturate the field with heterogeneity. "No 'local center,' no 'pattern of transformation' could function if, through a series of sequences, it did not eventually enter into an over-all strategy," he says. "And inversely, no strategy could achieve comprehensive effects if it did not gain support from precise and tenuous relations serving, not as its point of application or final outcome, but as its prop and anchor point" (99). There is neither discontinuity nor homogeneity between these two, but rather "the double conditioning of a strategy by the specificity of possible tactics, and of tactics by the strategic envelope that makes them work" (100).

In the language of eventalization, double conditioning "means rediscovering the connections, encounters, supports, blockage, plays of forces, strategies, and so on that at a given moment establish what subsequently counts as being self-evident, universal, and necessary. In this sense one is indeed effecting a sort of multiplication or pluralization of causes" (1987, 104). It means "analyzing an event according to the multiple processes that constitute it" (104), with a view both to the singularity one is examining and to that singularity's insertion into already existing practices comprising a larger, polymorphous field. This field will never be, simply, textual or discursive, in any narrow sense of these terms, but at each point, and across the network overall, will comprise a "double conditioning" of words and things, "of discourses, institutions, architectural forms, regulatory decisions, laws, administrative measures, scientific statements, philosophical, moral and philanthropic propositions—in short, the said as much as the unsaid" (1980, 194). This means that analysis of power, as of possibilities for change, will never forget the text. "We must make allowance," Foucault says, "for the complex and unstable process whereby discourse can be both an instrument and an effect of power, but also a hindrance, a stumbling-block, a point of resistance and a starting point for an opposing strategy" (1990, 101).

It seems to me that eventalization is the type of inquiry that Foucault initates in the concluding pages of The History of Sexuality, "Right of Death and Power over Life." White contends that in these pages Foucault succumbs to an enervating apocalypticism brought on by his discovery of the all-pervasiveness of power. Hope for the future is "dismissed as fatuous optimism" (1987, 131). Instead, "intimations of future biological wars and racial holocausts abound" (130–31). White emphasizes the theme of violent death, individual and social annhiliation, power's relentless vigilance that will cease only with final extinction: "Even the Nazis look tame in comparison with the 'bio-politics' that Foucault sees taking shape on the horizon," White writes. "He foresees an era of racial wars made more virulent than anything previously known in the degree to which 'knowledge' will have succeeded in internalizing, within the individual and the group, the play of 'sexuality' intended solely to discipline 'bodies and pleasures' "(133–34). I suggest that this is a misreading of Foucault's work. For, like the theorists of postmodernism I survey in the Introduction, White returns Foucault's writing to the repressive theory of power, and so to the dualistic language of inside and outside, executioner and victim, prohibition and counter-resistance. Foucault is not an apostle of doom—although some of his critics are. "I don't believe in the refrain of decadence," he remarks in a 1980 interview (1989c, 198). "I dream of a new age of curiosity" (199). Curiosity, Foucault explains, "evokes 'concern'; it evokes the care one takes for what exists and could exist" (198). It evokes a readiness to accept heterogeneity and the unfamiliar. Instead of "adopting a protectionist attitude, to prevent 'bad' information from invading and suffocating the 'good,' " he goes on to say, "we must multiply the paths and the possibility of comings and goings" (199).

In the concluding pages of *The History of Sexuality*, Foucault's eventalization proceeds along multiple paths, allowing for "the differentiation and simultaneity of different networks" (1989c, 199) through which our knowledges and practices form. Foucault's discussion in this section assumes a double-conditioning between, on the one hand, the *overall field* of power relations which, in the modern West, is bent on the generation, optimization, and administration of life; and on the other hand, the development of policy in *specific domains* such as nuclear technology, ecology, and medical and population genetics. From the early seventeenth to the late twentieth centuries, he suggests, the power of life and death is transferred from the right of the sovereign to the right of the social body. In the process, the sovereign right to life, once exercised as a power of deduction, a right to kill or refrain from killing, gives way to a network of power relations in which deduction is only one element among others which work together to generate and make grow, rather than to destroy or impede (1990, 136). Now, the power of death "presents itself as the counterpart of a power that exerts a positive influence on life, that endeavors to administer, optimize, and multiply it, subjecting it to precise controls and comprehensive regulations" (137). And now, it is not in the name of the sovereign but in the name of life necessity, in the name of the life of the social body, that one justifies the power to seize things and bodies, and ultimately, to take life itself.

Foucault cites the death penalty as an example of this transition taken from a specific domain. As the the power of life and death is transformed from its juridical to its modern life-generating forms, he says, justifications of the death penalty undergo a parallel transition. Once the power of life and death becomes aligned with the exigencies of life-administration, it becomes difficult to uphold the old justification for capital punishment: "How could power exercise its highest prerogatives by putting people to death, when its main role was to ensure, sustain, and multiply life, to put this life in order?" (138). Within an emerging field of power relations given to the production and optimization of life, capital punishment becomes a scandal which can no longer be maintained by invoking "the enormity of the crime itself" (138). Now it becomes necessary to link capital punishment to the life of the social body. It becomes necessary to appeal to "the monstrosity of the criminal, his incorrigibility, and the safeguard of society. One had the right to kill those who represented a kind of biological danger to others" (138). Justifications of the death penalty begin to relate it to the well-being of the social collective. At the same time, everyone is encouraged to see the punishment as in the interest of his or her own individual safety. This is one of the themes of *Discipline and Punish*.

The new network of mechanisms "working to incite, reinforce, control, monitor, optimize, and organize the forces under it" (136) takes death as power's limit: "the moment that escapes it; death becomes the most secret aspect of existence, the most 'private' "(138). But the modern power over life also brings with it an unprecedented power of death. Foucault points to the atomic situation as "at the end point" of a process through which technologies, developed in the name of defending the life of the social body, end up carrying "the power to expose a whole population to death" (137). Through a "turn that closes the circle" (137), new technologies, devised in the name of defending the life of the individual and the collective, harbor the power of all-out destruction—not just in the event of atomic or nuclear war, but through their insidious mutagenic and ecologically devastating potential. This two-sidedness characterizes those technologies which proliferated out of the so-called biological revolution of the 1950s and 1960s. Fostered as offering untold possibilities for the enhancement and preservation of life, and in some cases (for instance, anti-aging pills, cyrotechnology) as promising to ward off death altogether, these technologies also brought with them the potential for widepread destruction. It is to these technologies—these "bi-polar" power mechanisms centered on the human body, either as an "anatomo-politics" of the individual or as a "bio-politics of the population"—that Foucault turns in the concluding pages of this Introduction to his proposed analyses of the history of sexuality.

Bio-power is of interest to Foucault because here the deployment of sexuality is particularly at issue. His discussion in the last few pages of *The History of Sexuality* is highly suggestive of "eventalizing" analyses that could be done in any number of local centers. I am thinking, for example, of tactics, some of them eugenic, that developed simultaneously in medical genetics and population genetics around the concept of *genetic load*, tactics such as artificial insemination, freezing and banking of germ cells, *in vitro* fertilization, parthenogenesis, and prenatal diagnosis. Justification for use of these tactics followed the same argument, that of a biological threat to the population, as was adopted to support capital punishment. These tactics, too, were presented as necessary for the protection and enhancement of life.[6] In population and medical genetics, as in the case of capital punishment, the idea of a threat to the social body was posed as also an issue of individual self-interest, so much so that it was in the name of private rights—"[t]he 'right' to life, to one's body, to health, to happiness, to the satisfaction of needs" (1990, 145), and so on—that the societal demand for new reproductive technologies was made. Perhaps the most basic of these proliferating individual rights "was the 'right' to rediscover what one is and all that one can be" (145), the right to an unprecedented self-knowledge, which was supposed to be made available by techniques that could now penetrate the individual and social body even to the genetic and molecular levels.

I suggested earlier that for Foucault, historical analysis of power is always tied up with the development of contemporary strategies for change. Nowhere is this more evident than in these last pages of *The History of Sexuality* where he demonstrates, finally, that on the matter of change, his eventalization differs radically from a repressive analysis of power. For rather than locating (bio)technology in a position of exteriority to discourse as repressive theorists do (often while reiterating the language of rights), Foucault considers the rhetoric of individual/social rights to be itself a form of technique. Rather than invoking "rights" as a means of liberation from power, as what will bring technology under control, he considers rights too as belonging to bio-power's field. This does not mean that bio-power, for Foucault, is an all-encompassing closure, a determinism from which there is no escape. Within the overall field of contemporary bio-power, he says in "Right of Death and Power over Life," local centers of power-knowledge can maintain themselves only by invoking the justification of "freedom from" that characterizes the contemporary discourse of private rights. But such discourse, he emphasizes, serves power as *both* support *and* opposition. Resistances are not located outside, but are present everywhere inside discursive networks: individualist rights-discourse *both* facilitates the technological system *and* permeates it with points of resistance: "Discourse transmits and produces power; it reinforces it, but also undermines and exposes it, renders it fragile and makes it possible to thwart it" (101).

Beginning from local centers, then, rather than attempting to take on the field of bio-power overall, eventalizing analyses would look for points of resistance which render bio-power fragile, perhaps along those *fault lines* within the discourse of rights where, even as the circle closes here too, differences appear that are already inscribed on the surface of the discourse itself. The task of eventalization, Foucault says, is one of trying to understand "the nature of the present, and of 'ourselves in the present' " (1988a, 36). This task has been important to philosophy at least since Kant's *Was ist Aufklärung?*, he suggests. The task does not consist in a simple characterization of what we "are," but rather by following "lines of fragility in the present" it attempts "to grasp why and how that-which-is might no longer be that-which-is" (36). Hayden White is correct in noting that rights are not "natural" for Foucault, and that if "Foucault seems to be defending the individual against society, it is not because he credits any idea of natural rights or the sanctity of a contract between the members of society, or between them and their government" (1987, 128). For Foucault, rights are precisely what need to be examined as the historically and culturally specific theoretical correlate of modern technique. Rather than championing the rights of the individual over against those of society, his analyses take rights to be constitutive of an individual/society dualism through which we define "ourselves in the present." This approach "provides a starting point where the couple

'individual' and 'society' no longer constrains the questions posed because from the outset it is problematized" (Henriques et al. 1984, 100).

It may be that Foucault's mode of problematization is nowhere more
relevant today than in the context of the discursive incitement generated
by AIDS. It is not the case, as Judith Butler suggests, that in *The History of
Sexuality*, Foucault "sought to separate sex from death by announcing the
end of the era in which death reigns"; that he "did not consider that the
regulatory discourse on sex could itself produce death, pronounce death,
even proliferate it"; and therefore, that his analysis in the book needs rewriting now "in light of the power/discourse regime that regulates AIDS"
(Butler 1993, 96, 83). On the contrary, *The History of Sexuality* presents
modern power over life as the counterpart of a formidable power of death, a
power exercised precisely through regulatory discourses on sex—such as
the discourses that regulate AIDS. The type of analysis proposed in the
book would not exclude these regulatory discourses from consideration as
sites of viral transmission. For instance, when AIDS is portrayed as occas-
ioning a clash between personal rights and public health, and when prevention of spread of the virus is said to require a seizure of "rights" from the
carrier, who, like the criminal to be executed, is said to pose a biological
threat to other individuals and to the collective, not the sought-for containment but proliferation can be the result. Particularly in the 1980s, a
negative, "freedom from threat," argument was used to support calls for
breach of confidentiality, widespread identification of carriers, restricted
public access, and even quarantine, although from very early on in the
course of the epidemic, these measures had been demonstrated to be not
only ineffective in preventing spread of the virus, but also counter-preventive. The point is that in eventalizing analyses, the "object" to be "controlled" is never simply "outside" of discourse. Foucault studies the history
of sexuality within an analysis of power that does not remove either
"power" or "sex" from the text.

Ascesis

The History of Sexuality appeared in 1976, but it was 1984 before Foucault
published the second two volumes in the sexuality series, *L'Usage des
plaisirs* (*The Use of Pleasure*) and *Le Souci de soi* (*The Care of the Self*).
During the eight-year gap, he doubled back from modern Western societies to ancient Greece and Rome, a turn made necessary, he said, by the

question of "the subject" that was increasingly raised for him by his historical studies of sexuality, the question of how and why "the individual constitutes himself *qua* subject" (1985, 6). It occurred to him that "one could not very well analyze the formation and development of the experience of sexuality from the eighteenth century onward, without doing a historical and critical study dealing with desire and the desiring subject" (5). How did it happen in a given period that individuals came to constitute themselves as sexual subjects, so as to link sex and the search for the truth, the secret of the human self? And through what processes had the desiring subject become an object of ethical concern? Realizing that he "could only produce this *History of Sexuality* adequately by retracing what happened in antiquity to see how sexuality was manipulated, lived, and modified by a certain number of actors" (1988c, 252; see also 1983), Foucault gave up, for the time being, his early-to-late-modern focus, and decided to begin again.

In the tropological space of his work which, he once remarked, "takes place between unfinished abutments and lines of dots" (1987, 101), this spiralling back and starting over is not uncharacteristic. It might even be Foucault's signature, for not only did he invariably begin to write without "knowing in advance what I wanted to do and where I wanted to go"—an open strategy which he related to "the ethics of an intellectual" (1989b, 303)—but also, his life ended before he arrived: Foucault's death in 1984 left the sexuality series unfinished with a fourth volume, *Les Aveux de la chair* (*Confessions of the Flesh*) unpublished. Didier Eribon suggests that Foucault's proposed history of sexuality "was transformed over the years by the ups and downs of a 'logic of discovery,' in which hesitations and mistakes, bad habits, and moments of repentance played their role, before being overcome and surpassed by new intuitions and new discoveries" (1991, 318–19). Eribon outlines some of these ups and downs: Foucault's comment to Hubert Dreyfus and Paul Rabinow in 1983 that there would be only two volumes of his history of sexuality; his decision, shortly after that, to integrate these two history of sexuality volumes with a collection of studies of the self; his toying with the possibility of bringing it all together in one big book; his discouragement at the rumors generated by the delay in publication, even his speaking on a number of occasions of abandoning writing altogether; and at the same time, his determination to have the project finished (319–22). But this zigzagging, wandering, back-and-forth movement is not peculiar to Foucault's last two books. The sexuality series began the same way,

volume 1 remaining untitled "right up to the last moment," and undergo-
ing several successive drafts, in some of which, Foucault said, he "turned
the whole thing upside down" and attempted a different line of approach
(1980, 209–10). The modification of assumptions and the shaking-up of
conventional ways of working and thinking, were always part of
Foucault's writing style.[7]

Perhaps not too much should be made, then, of the so-called stylis-
tic break that takes place between *The History of Sexuality* and Foucault's
last two volumes, *The Use of Pleasure* and *The Care of the Self*. "Foucault's
writing changed a great deal in his last two books," Eribon remarks (331).
Yes, but his writing was always changing, so much so that one book might
seem to be at cross purposes with the previous ones, and just as well,
Foucault said, for: "that would show that my own undertaking is at cross
purposes" (1980, 196). That would show that Foucault himself was moti-
vated by the kind of curiosity he called *ethical*, "not the curiosity that
seeks to assimilate what it is proper for one to know, but that which
enables one to get free of oneself" (1985, 8). This kind of curiosity generated his catachretic style, his manner of working "down" (G *kata*: de-
noting motion from above, down from), "gropingly, and by means of
different or successive fragments" (11), not in order to arrive at an underlying secret, but in an endeavor to trace, through the labyrinth of historical texts, the twisting, enfolding paths of knowledge, power and pleasure.
In his introduction to *The Use of Pleasure* (8–11), Foucault uses the vocabulary of the "tropological space" of *Death and the Labyrinth* to describe
philosophy as what he calls *ascesis*, or "*askesis*, an exercise of oneself in
the activity of thought" (9). *Ascesis* asks whether "one can think differently than one thinks, and perceive differently than one sees" (8). It implies a willingness "to alter one's way of looking at things, to change the
boundaries of what one knows and to venture out a ways from there"
(11). It results in "the knower's straying afield of himself" (8). This is
Foucault's autograph.

And it would be this catachretic signature, this *ascesis*, rather than
the autobiographical revelation of a kind of *chresis*, that makes Foucault's
work important for ethics. Foucault says in *The Use of Pleasure* that the
Greeks related the term *chresis aphrodision* to an individual's management
of his sexual activity, to the use or enjoyment of one's pleasure, not according to a binary of permitted and forbidden, but according to a strategy of moderation or "principle of stylization of conduct for those who
wished to give their existence the most graceful and accomplished form

possible" (251). His analysis of this "aesthetics of existence" has already proven significant in opening up new lines of inquiry for historians and classicists.[8] It has also led to suggestions that such a stylization of exist- ence was attempted by Foucault himself.

For instance, Simon During argues that through the sexuality series, Foucault's work took an "aesthetic turn," as he came "to concede that the space of contestation in our culture is not primarily linguistic," but rather the space of "individual 'self-governmentality'," not "transgressive writ- ing," but "the space of private liberty in which the individual has room to work on him or herself rather than be worked on by others" (During 1992, 11–12). In Foucault's last books, During claims, the ethical and the transgressive are, at least to some extent, reconciled, as Foucault comes to view "[t]he ability to create one's own lifestyle . . . to shape an aesthet- ics of existence" as a space of freedom within a society increasingly domi- nated by the concept of "normality," and as he comes to accept what he had already realized in the book on Roussel, "that a way of writing is also a manner of living" (12). Hayden White makes a similar suggestion when he says that it was "to elaborate the notion of style and especially the notion of a 'style of life' " (1987, 135) that Foucault turned from the modern "science of sex" to classical Greece and Rome. Still concerned with "the folly displayed in every 'will to know' " (137), Foucault returns in the last two books to the question of style that had occupied him in his book on Roussel. In *Death and the Labyrinth*, Foucault "praised Roussel for his 'reversed style'," White says. Now, "[i]n his account of the Classical discourse of sexuality, he appears to fault the ancients for their failure to develop a similarly reversed style in the cultivation of their pleasures" (138–39). The (catachretic) irony, for White, is that this "faulting of the ancients" for failing to develop a reversed style is presented by Foucault in two stylistically conventional texts: "Would it not be height of irony for a scholar known for his idiosyncratic style in his early works to end his career by the composition of at least two books in which what was written was 'straight' history, in which the method used was the most conventional kind of philological analysis, and in which the manner of composition was so pedantic as to make of sex the most boring of subjects?" (140).

I leave White here, where his essay ends, positing the irony of "straight" history coming from the likes of Foucault. White's comment may or may not be a veiled reference to Foucault's homosexuality: the "secret" revealed only after his death, but encoded within the "reversed style" that he took from his "hero," Roussel. In any case, suggestions that Foucault's catachresis eventuated in a "transgressive" life style are easy enough to come by (Kroker's *The Possessed Individual* is another case in point). My argument is that these suggestions either reduce or cancel the significance of his writing for ethics. They can, moreover, only add support to calls for coercive and counter-preventive measures for containment of AIDS. It is not Foucault's "life-style" that is important for discussions of ethics and of ethical policies for prevention of AIDS, but rather, his "monstrous" *ascesis*, his writing style itself, as a catachretic practice. Catachresis, Derrida suggests, is "another kind of writing, a violent writing, which stakes out the faults (*failles*) and deviations of language, so that the text produces a language of its own, in itself, which while continuing to work through tradition emerges at a given moment as a monster, a monstrous mutation without tradition or normative precedent" (Derrida 1984a, 123). Catachresis, so understood, is what "the French" call *ethical writing*, a style of historical analysis which looks for lines of fragility and knots of resistance that are spread over the great surface network of words and things. Foucault's catachresis does not attempt the dissolution of discourse through the unveiling of something hidden. Rather, by following surface fault lines, it attempts to practice reading and writing as other than what we have taken these to be. The opening to difference is what makes catachresis ethical: it offers a chance "to think otherwise, to do something else, to become other than what one is" (Foucault 1989c, 201).

Notes

Introduction

1. As I expect will become clear during the course of this introduction, by putting the designator "French" in quotation marks, I am attempting to open the term to the test of translation. For what Lyotard (chapter 2) calls a "politics of forgetting"—a practice of representation that closes off heterogeneity or *le différend*—is at work in the theorizing of postmodernism as a Franco-American narrative. I am suggesting the need to "deconstruct," to open to differences, the rigid national, political, linguistic, theoretical and sexual boundaries that this narrative puts in place. I am suggggesting the need to open to something other than critics such as Kroker and Jameson do when they use the designator without quotation marks. The issue of "contamination" is also relevant here, in that all (national, political, linguistic, theoretical, sexual) designators are already divided by internal difference(s): "the French" are never simply or purely "French," and as Derrida points out, the "American" scene is "always more than the American scene." See my discussion of this later in the introduction.

2. I'll settle for this as a definition of what Kroker means by *panic*: "*all text, no sex*" (Kroker and Kroker 1987, 18). Panic reality is *virtual*, a cyber-reality from which matter (body) is missing.

3. In *Of Spirit: Heidegger and the Question*, for instance, Derrida reads Heidegger's discourse on technology as maintaining the possibility of an essential thinking that is protected from any contamination by the technology about which it thinks. But such thought or speech of

the essence is "originarily" impurified or contamined by technology, Derrida argues. "Contamination, then, of the thought of the essence by technology, and so contamination by technology of the thinkable essence of technology" (1989b, 10). Contamination would also be of Kroker's thought of the virtual. I pick up on this issue of contamination later in the Introduction.

4. See Paul Bové's "The Foucault Phenomenon" (in Deleuze 1986), which suggests that Jameson's anxiety "is about identity and propriety: anxious to differentiate the 'synchronic' from the Marxist, the legitimately authorized intellectual from the usurping conservative and nihilist pretenders, his text stops its own critical dialectic in a way that reveals the workings of academic power upon the limits of oppositional theory and practice" (xxiv).

5. One reason why Jameson is more sympathetic to structuralism than to poststructuralism in both *The Prison House of Language* and "Periodizing the 60s" (1988b) may be, as Geoff Bennington and Robert Young suggest, that "'difference,' as understood by post-structuralism, is incompatible with orthodox formulations of the dialectic as much as it is with traditional absolutes, and therefore necessarily comes into conflict with classical Marxism in a way in which structuralism did not" (1987, 5).

6. What makes his method "political," Jameson says, is that it works "from within" postmodernism rather than assuming a transcendent position of moral judgment. But I am taking issue with Jameson's claim, and suggest that his analysis of postmodernism constitutes a "thought of the essence" as much as Kroker's does. See note 3 above.

7. Thus for Jameson, "only the dialectic provides a way for 'decentering' the subject concretely, and for transcending the 'ethical' in the direction of the political and the collective" (1981, 60).

8. See also Hassan's "The Question of Postmodernism" and "Pluralism in Postmodern Perspective." His definition of postmodernism also resolves in a call for a consensus, for a return to shared values.

9. Kearney's *poetics of the possible*, would "discriminate between the authentic and inauthentic aspects of postmodern culture" ("Ethics and the Postmodern Imagination" 43). It would be committed to "the invention of a new social project" (44). See also Kearney's "The Crisis of the Postmodern Image."

10. Another *post-*ing: the word "poststructrualism," like "postmodernism," was unknown in France until its return there from the United States, Derrida suggests in his "Letter to a Japanese Friend" (3).

11. Jameson, on the other hand, would have Lyotard returning us to the past. See his foreword to *The Postmodern Condition*, which argues that "Lyotard is in reality quite unwilling to posit a postmodernist stage radically different from the period of high modernism and involving a fundamental cultural break with this last." Rather, "although he has polemically endorsed the slogan of a 'postmodernism' and has been involved in the defense of some of its more controversial productions," Lyotard ultimately concurs with his rival Habermas, in that "for both of them a return to the older critical high modernism is still possible" (xvi–xvii).

12. Stephen Slemon says that "the only point of consensus in the debate over 'postmodernism' is that the defining term of this apparently contemporary phenomenon inherently posits for Euro-American culture some kind of radical break from the discourse of 'modernism' as it developed at the end of the nineteenth century" (1990, 1). Such positing of a consensus as to what postmodernism *is* enables critics to get on with the question of the "future direction of the new development as such" (Suleiman 1991, 113). This is one way in which periodization serves the narrative of progress and the impulse to gain time.

13. Hutcheon writes in *The Politics of Postmodernism* that "[t]he difference between the postmodern and the feminist can be seen in the potential quietism of the political ambiguities or paradoxes of postmodernism. The many feminist social agendas demand a theory of agency, but such a theory is visibly lacking in postmodernism, caught as it is in a certain negativity that may be inherent in any critique of cultural dominants. It has no theory of postive action on a social level" (22).

14. On the need to formulate a social project, and on this as the meaning of change, Hutcheon seems to agree with Kroker, Suleiman, and Jameson. For Jameson, "the thematics of feminism do not have to be taken as an alternate interpretive code," that is, an alternative to his own, "provided we are united, if not by some achieved vision of a future Utopian community, then at least by the necessity of developing one" (Jameson 1982, 91).

1. Deconstruction's Delirium

1. The conference proceedings, including Derrida's essay (445–79), have been published under the conference title, *Les fins de l'homme: à*

partir du travail de Jacques Derrida (ed. Lacoue-Labarthe and Nancy). I have followed John Leavey's English translation of Derrida's essay, which appears in *Semeia* 23 (1982): 63–97. Derrida's essay also appears in English in *The Oxford Literary Review* 6.2 (1984): 3–37 and in *Raising the Tone of Philosophy* (ed. Peter Fenves), 117–71.

2. Peter Fenves' English translation of Kant's essay appears in *Raising the Tone of Philosophy*, 51–81.

3. Kant's immediate target in "Of an Overlordly Tone" is the annotated translation of Plato's *Letters* by Johan Georg Schlosser, but, more generally, he directs his polemic against a widespread "Plato-enthusiasm" and Christian sentimentalism (see Fenves 1993, 72–75).

4. "With what is a tone, a change or rupture of tone marked?," Derrida asks in his Cerisy paper (1982b, 66) where, as in all of his writing, play with the resonances of the *etymon* ("the meaningful play of the slippage of the *etymon*" [Nancy 1992, 41]) both upsets (*délirer*) the linear order of reading and "untunes" or "slackens" reference, that is, constitutes an errance of the name from the thing. Such slackening also contributes to the tonal displacements opened by Derrida when he follows a "thread" through several texts. In its attention to *timbre*, for instance, "Of an Apocalyptic Tone" weaves back and forth across Derrida's earlier and later readings, in particular, "Tympan" (in *Margins of Philosophy*), *Glas*, "No Apocalypse, Not Now (full speed ahead, seven missiles, seven missives)," and *Cinders*. This weaving in and out is a double movement ("an apocalyptic movement") which, *on the one hand*, links "*timbre (tympanum), style*, and *signature*" within "the same obliterating division of the proper" ("Tympan," xix), and on the other hand, opens the text (L *textus*, pattern or style of weaving; a woven fabric f. *texo, texere*, to weave or baste) to its *espacement*. Thus, Derrida's writing is less "bound" than "basted," as Alan Bass suggests (translator's introduction, *Writing and Difference*, xiii).

5. Derrida, in *Positions* (22): "*Phone*, in effect, is the signifying substance given to consciousness as that which is most intimately tied to the thought of the signified concept. From this point of view, the voice is consciousness itself. When I speak, not only am I conscious of being present for what I think, but I am conscious also of keeping as close as possible to my thought, or to the 'concept,' a signifier that does not fall into the world, a signifier that I hear as soon as I emit it, that seems to depend upon my pure and free spontaneity, requiring the use of no instrument, no accessory, no force taken from the world."

6. A man who is deaf from birth, Kant writes in his *Anthropology* (34), "can never achieve more than an *analogue* of reason." But can the deaf use the other senses vicariously? "If a deaf man was once able to hear, we can get him to speak as he used to by gesturing to him, and so by means of his eyes. He can also use his eyes to read our lips, or his sense of touch to feel our lip movements in the dark. If however, he has been deaf from birth, his sense of *sight* must begin with movements of the vocal organs and convert the sounds he has been taught to make into a feeling of moving the muscles of his own vocal organs. But he never *arrives* [my italics] at real concepts this way, because the signs he uses are not the sort that can be universalized. . . . Which lack or loss of a sense is more serious, deafness or blindness? If a man is born deaf, hearing is the least replaceable of all the senses" (37–38). See "Economimesis" (19–20) for Derrida's analysis of the auto-affective structure of this passage.

7. Freud's signature is at issue in "Coming into One's Own," where Derrida considers that portion of the second chapter of *Beyond the Pleasure Principle* in which Freud recounts the narrative of the reel and of the *fort:da*. The text is *autobiographical*, Derrida suggests, since Freud, the witness to the experiment, is also the grandfather of Ernst, the child who repeatedly dispatches and calls back the reel (which is supposed to represent the mother, Freud's daughter, Sophie). Freud writes the autobiography as a "contract with himself," Derrida argues, a contract which leaves him "holding all the strings of his line, descendants and ascendants, in an incontestable ascendancy" (134). For Freud, like the child he observes, plays *fort:da* with the Pleasure Principle (PP), repeatedly summoning back the hypothesis of something beyond the Pleasure Principle only to dismiss it, and so to retain the mastery of the *pépé* (the grandfather, Freud). Derrida's deconstructive reading transforms this autobiography-as-science, this establishment of psychoanalysis as a science based on return to the PP and so to the grand speculating father, Freud, the *pépé* ("a postal money order sent to himself" [143]), into an auto(bio)graphical scene of writing. ("Coming into One's Own" is printed in *The Post Card* as "Freud's Legacy," 292–337).

8. It's this very "contamination," I suppose we could say, that Jameson continues to rail against today when he laments the "collapse" of "tradition" and the mixing of "philosophy" with "theory."

9. The quotation, taken from Spivak, grafts the subtitle of Derrida's "Géopsychanalyse: 'and the rest of the world' " (see Spivak 1984, 20).

10. In the process of being posted to North America from France, deconstruction was cut off from its "traditional" and "philosophical" roots. It entered the North American academy through literary studies, and was for the most part ignored by departments of philosophy. And as Anthony Appiah remarks, "because the mainstream philosophy of the anglophone world—analytic philosophy—has refused to recognize its legitimacy—insisting, as often as not, on its essential foreignness—deconstruction has been allowed to settle here only on the condition of internal exile" (Appiah 1986, 49).

11. Like Kant, Howey, the philosopher, lampoons the mystagogue's overlordly tone: "Surely, all of this is a bad joke which has gone awry, in that such gibberish has been taken seriously and influenced minds which might be better occupied watching television" (Howey 1985, 90).

12. See for example, Somer Brodribb's reading of Derrida in *Nothing Mat(t)ers*, 71–87. For a discussion of deconstruction's implications for feminist ethics and women's studies, see "Women in the Beehive," especially Derrida's remark that "The effect of the Law is to build the structure of the subject, and as soon as you say, 'well, the woman is a subject and this subject deserves equal rights,' and so on—then you are caught in the logic of phallogocentrism and you have rebuilt the empire of the Law. So it seems that women's studies can't go very far if it does not deconstruct the philosophical framework of this situation, starting with the notion of subject, of ego, of consciousness, soul and body, and so on" (1987c, 193).

13. See, in particular, "Living On: Borderlines," Derrida's reading of Maurice Blanchot's *L'arrêt de mort*, and "At this very moment in this work here I am," a response by Derrida to Levinas.

14. "The sacred text marks the limit . . . the ideal starting from which one could think, evaluate, measure the essential, that is to say poetic, translation," Derrida says in "Des Tours de Babel" (202). And it is as a measure of the poetic and mystagogic, rather than the theologic, that Derrida appeals to the Johannine Apocalypse in "Of an Apocalyptic Tone." See both "Des Tours de Babel" and "How To Avoid Speaking: Denials," where Derrida deals with the question why deconstruction is not (negative) theology.

15. We might say that Kant's conceptual oppositions not only *call* for deconstruction, but that "they deconstruct themselves, even as paradigms for deconstruction" (Derrida 1992a, 38).

16. Derrida's comment on this point in "Passions" (13–14) needs citing at length:

> One can attend or participate today, in many different places, in a congenial and disturbing task: to restore morality and especially to reassure those who had serious reasons for being troubled by this topic. Some minds believing themselves to have found in Deconstruction ['*La Deconstruction*'], as if there were only one, a modern form of immorality, of amorality or of irresponsibility (etc.: a discourse too well known, I do not need to continue), while others, more serious, in less of a hurry, better disposed towards so-called Deconstruction, today claim the opposite; they discern encouraging signs and in increasing numbers (at times, I must admit, in some of my texts) which would testify to a permanent, extreme, direct or oblique, in any event, increasingly intense attention, to those things which one could identify under the fine names of 'ethics,' 'morality,' 'responsibility,' 'subject,' etc. Before reverting to not-responding, I would like to declare in the most direct way that if I had the *sense* of duty and responsibility, it would compel me to break with both of these moralisms, with these two restorations of morality, including, therefore, the remoralization of deconstruction which naturally seems to me more attractive than that to which it is rightly opposed, but which at each moment risks reassuring itself in order to reassure the other and to promote the consensus of a new dogmatic slumber. And it is so that one not be in too much of a hurry to say that it is in the name of a higher responsibility and a more intractable [*intraitable*] moral exigency that I declare my distaste, uneven as it may be, for both moralisms.

17. I am reminded here of Derrida's opening remarks to a 1984 Cornell University colloquium on nuclear criticism, his warning, dissuasion, or deceleration, offered in the form of an apostrophe: "*Watch out, don't go too fast.*" Speaking on this occasion of one of the most serious, we might say the most apocalyptic, of subjects, he chooses, typically, to play, giving his paper the title, "No Apocalypse, Not Now (full speed ahead, seven missiles, seven missives)," and adopting for its structure "the genre or rhetorical form of tiny atomic nuclei (in the process of fission or division in an uninterruptable chain)" which

he projects toward his audience "like tiny inoffensive missiles: in a discontinuous, more or less haphazard fashion" (21). Derrida's paper mimes the technics of nuclear emissions, but as is the case in his Cerisy paper, the strategy, playful but not frivolous, is "to mime in citation but also to transform in kind" (65), to read the discourse of nuclear criticism so as to effect a transformation or *iteration* of the prevailing understanding of the text. His deconstructive reading of nuclear criticism (which, he suggests, bears more than a homonymy with Kantian criticism) uncovers the same binaries (same/different, inside/outside, literal/figural, competent/incompetent, etc.) that structure "Of an Overlordly Tone." But at the same time, in Derrida's reading, nuclear discourse (with its multiplicity of addressees and senders and the inseparability it demonstrates between fact and doxa, concept and metaphor, *technē* and text) turns out to be an exemplary revelation of the apocalyptic scene of writing. The rationalist and realist discourse of nuclear deterrence proves also to be a logic of dissemination and disinterrence.

2. Arrive-t-il?

1. The *post* as *postponement*, deferral to the other, figures in both Derrida's and Lyotard's work. See for this Derrida's "How To Avoid Speaking: Denials."

2. When Lyotard says that no ready-made subject takes it place *before* the phrase, he has an ethical subject in mind. Like Derrida (whose "Come" cannot come from an identifiable someone), Lyotard insists that an ethical subject cannot *come before us* as model or demand.

3. The issue of contamination (see chapter 1) comes up again here, brought on by the "fact" that every "entity" is always "in excess" of what we represent it to be.

4. In what might be the best pages of *Heidegger and "the jews"*, Lyotard relates the Freudian *Nachträglichkeit* to the West's construction of sexual difference. See 19–20.

5. Another point on which there seems to be agreement between Lyotard and Derrida concerns this matter of the "political" significance of *Dasein's* pro-jection. See for example, Derrida's reading of Heidegger in *Of Spirit*, in "*Geschlecht*: Sexual Difference, Ontological Difference," and in "*Geschlecht* II: Heidegger's Hand."

6. One of these is the case of the Ibanskian witness. Either he is or he is not a communist. If he is a communist, he has no right to question whether the Ibanskian society is communist. He must agree with the communist authorities, since only they are allowed to judge what communism really is. If the witness disagrees with these authorities, he ceases to be a communist and his testimony is again dismissed (Lyotard 1988a, 4). Another example is the case of Faurisson. He claims to have been fooled about the so-called Final Solution and demands that a witness come forward who can furnish acceptable proof of the reality of the Nazi gas chambers. Lyotard summarizes his argument as follows: "in order for a place to be identified as a gas chamber, the only eyewitness I will accept would be a victim of the gas chamber; now, according to my opponent, there is no victim that is not dead; otherwise, this gas chamber would not be what he or she claims it to be. There is, therefore, no gas chamber" (3–4). There are other examples.

7. Geoff Bennington points out that in *The Differend*, "taking Plato's dialogues as his exemplary text, Lyotard suggests that the peculiarity of philosophy is to position a figure of the disciple in the text, thus controlling the essential unpredictability of the addressee's response by prefiguring it in the statement. Philosophy offers a model of its right reader, and this leads to the creation of a space of the School or the University. Philosophy would have us believe that such discipline is simply an indispensable preliminary to the practice of its genre: Lyotard replies that this positioning is immanent to the text of philosophy and not prior to it as a propedeutic—in an attempt to challenge this set-up, *Le Différend* will define its reader as 'philosophical, i.e., anyone at all' " (1988, 118).

8. The "Result" section of *The Differend* (86–106) was originally presented as "Discussions, ou: phraser 'après Auschwitz' " at the same Cerisy-la-Salle colloquium at which Derrida delivered "Of an Apocalyptic Tone." The French version of Lyotard's original paper is published in the conference proceedings, *Les fins de l'homme: à partir du travail de Jacques Derrida* (283–315). An English translation of the paper, including Lyotard's transcription of the discussion which followed its delivery at Cerisy-la-Salle, appears in *The Lyotard Reader* (360–92).

9. The burden of Lyotard's demonstration, Bennington suggests, "is not that speculative discourse is wrong, but that it is one genre among

others, with rules that can be formulated. This already undermines its claim to speak the truth of all other genres and to discover a necessity in sentence-links in general. For Lyotard, it is not that speculative discourse is 'wrong' in the sense of being incorrect, but in the sense of being unjust" (1988, 136).

10. For both Derrida and Lyotard, the ethical is inseparable from this apostrophe, this call that cannot come from an identifiable subject, that cannot be "heard" as prosposition or project, but yet to which we are obliged to respond.

11. This idea of a response that turns the subject around will come up again with Lacan. See the discussion of the "analytic trope" in chapter 3.

12. Lyotard's essay was first published in *Paragraph* 11.1 (March 1988): 1–23. Translated by Marian Hobson and Geoff Bennington.

13. But how would Kant's "interior music" relate to Heidegger's "subjective interiority," and to all the tonal modalities (*Stimmung, Bestimmung, Übereinstimmung, Verstimmen, Verstimmtheit, Verstimmung,* etc.) that Derrida reads, deconstructively, in "Heidegger's Ear"?

14. Lyotard's analysis of the "failure" or "fault" of Heideggerian deconstruction extends in *Heidegger and "the jews"* to a critique of deconstructive readings of Heidegger, in particular those of Derrida and Philippe Lacoue-Labarthe, and more broadly, to a critique of "the very fault of deconstruction, in itself" (76), a critique that David Carroll considers at some length in his foreword to the book. One implication of Lyotard's reading in "Sensus Communis" may be that what he takes to be "too respectfully nihilist" (1990, 75) about Derrida's work is its "silence" on the euphonious "pre-subject" that comes "before" deconstruction. On the other hand, Lyotard's "naming" of this "pre-subject," his "positioning" of it in the "place" of the "before," may be too-nearly "pious" for Derrida, too close to a predestination. The matter, in any case, requires more careful analysis than I can give it here.

15. I am not tracing out the relation between this aesthetics and political judgement, which is something that has already been done by others, notably David Carroll, especially in *Paraesthetics*.

3. Soulmorality

1. There is an extraordinary passage in *The Sayings of the Fathers* (Chadwick 1958, 65–66) which indicates how, on its other side, the Christian idealization of the body of the virgin turns into abjection of woman-in-the-flesh:

> A brother was tested by temptation in Scete. And the enemy sent to his soul the memory of a fair woman, and troubled him sorely. And by God's providence it chanced that another brother came down from Egypt and arrived in Scete. And when they met to talk, he told him that his wife was dead (she was the woman about whom he was being disturbed). When he heard the news, he put on his cloak in the night and went to the place where he had heard she was buried. And he dug the place, and wiped the blood of her corpse on his cloak, and kept it in his cell when he returned. And when it smelt too much, he put it in front of him and hurriedly said to his temptation: "Look, this is what you desire. You have it now, fill yourself." And so he chastised himself with the smell until his passions died down.

2. In *The Living Theatre of Medieval Art*, Henry Kraus takes twelfth-century sculpted reliefs of the deadly Vice of Unchastity to be representations of the Christian antitype of Mary, woman as temptress, as Eve. The Vice is invariably portrayed as a woman suffering eternally in hell, Kraus says. "She is usually shown in a revolting posture, her naked body entwined with serpents which feed on her breasts and sexual organs. Sometimes, too, she is accompanied by the Devil, who assumes an intimate relationship to her" (42). One particular relief above the door of a fourteenth-century monastery at Chartreuse-du-Val-de-Bénédiction shows a wild and obscene woman, recumbent, and in a scabrous position with a goat. Kraus: "Not aimed at the public but at a single pair of cloistered eyes, what could its message be other than a warning against woman's bestiality, meant to rally the monks' resistance at faltering moments?" (41).

3. In his "Translator's Note," Heath says not only that "English lacks a word able to carry the range of meaning in the term *jouissance*," but also that Barthes contrasts the *jouissance* of *Image Music Text* to the

plaisir of his *Plaisir du texte*: "on the one hand a pleasure (*plaisir*) linked to cultural enjoyment and identity, to the cultural enjoyment of identity, to a homogenizing movement of the ego; on the other a radically violent pleasure (*jouissance*) which shatters—dissipates, loses—that cultural identity, that ego" (9). That Barthes' use of *jouissance* in *Image Music Text* brings with it the same connotations of the rupturing of ego as are suggested by Lacan in *Encore*, makes Heath's translation all the more curious, all the more confident.

4. For two very different accounts of Lacan's concept of the subject as being at the core of his controversy with orthodox psychoanalysis, see Ragland-Sullivan 1987, 5–6 and Weber 1991, 99–100.

5. As Anthony Wilden points out, Lacan's views on the mirror stage evolved and therefore cannot be presented *en bloc* (1968, 182). From 1936 until about 1953, Wilden says, Lacan concentrated on the *genetic view*: "here he is concerned about the *stade du miroir* as a specific phase in development." In later works, "Lacan's emphasis becomes almost exclusively structural, and he concentrates upon the logical level of the *chaîne signifiante* in an attempt to construct a 'logic of the signifier' on the basis of the child's earliest relation to objects" (162).

6. "This myth can only ever be mythical precisely because any knowledge that one has of the processes pre-existing language and the unconscious are known only through language and its symbolic relations" (Coward and Ellis 1977, 101).

7. And yet, the subject, "born" divided as a result of this narcissistic illusion, should not be conceived of as a unity prior to the mirror stage. For Lacan, the human creature, being a creature of biological drives, is originarily submitted to the divisions of matter. Even before birth, there is already "a certain dehiscence at the heart of the organism, a primordial Discord" (1977a, 4). The mirror stage is not a "fall" from wholeness into language and (as) difference.

8. According to Weber, the future anterior tense, in which all of Lacan's work is inscribed, makes impossible a simple return to the "original" text of *le stade du miroir*. "In returning to the mirror stage," Weber says, "it should come as no shock that we do not go back to the *same place*: to the immutable *topos* of an unaltered text, but rather to another place and to other texts, even if they appear under the same title" (101–2).

9. These lines are taken from E. Récéjac's *Essai sur les fondements de la Connaissance Mystique* (Paris: 1897), as cited in Underhill 1955, 82.

10. Underhill says that the "One is for the mystic, not merely the Reality of all that is, but also a living and personal Object of Love" (1955, 81). "Living union with this One" which, she says, is the goal of the mystic's adventure, "is arrived at by an arduous psychological and spiritual process—the so-called Mystic Way" (81).

11. Rudolph Bell notes that Teresa "regularly used an olive twig to induce vomiting so that she might receive the host without fear of rejecting it" (18). Yet as far as her "holy anorexia" is concerned, she seems to have fared better than many other brides of Christ, whose self-starvation and sacrificial mutilation (see Schulenburg 1986) led to traumatic early death. Can it be, then, as Evelyn Underhill suggests (1955, 137), that only a "prurient imagination" would confuse such "morbid" details with the "unearthly vision" of the virgin soul in a union of likeness with Christ? Insistent that spiritual marriage not be contaminated by a "physical" or "sensuous" reading, Underhill finds the nuptial imagery in the mystic text to be "annointed and ordained to a holy office, carried up, transmuted, and endowed with a radiant purity, an intense and spiritual life" (137). Underhill, too, transcendentalizes the bridal soul into a place "utterly beyond the resources of speech" (426) where, through "spiritual motherhood," even the bride's "reproductive power" is invested in the ideal (432).

    Dietrich von Hildebrand's *In Defense of Purity* also idealizes the already-idealizing discourse of spiritual marriage, and in so doing, the book reinstates, rather than undercuts, the binary order of sexual difference. Von Hildebrand argues that the mystic's soul is feminine because "[i]n the natural order woman represents, in contrast to the man, the receptive principle," and so is "the natural image of the soul as receptive or conceiving from and by Christ" (88). On the other hand, "the male is in the spiritual sphere," thus retains the power of creation, generation, and signification, and is "better fitted to fulfil in the supernatural order also the giving function of the priest as the representative of Christ" (88).

4. *L'Écriture limite*

1. The technical language of this early essay serves perhaps as a reminder that the young literary critic, newly arrived in France, had at one time wanted to go to Duobno in Siberia to become an astrono-

mer or a physicist. Kristeva speaks of her interest in becoming a scientist in "Julia Kristeva: à quoi servent les intellectuels?," an interview with Jean-Paul Enthoven, where she also responds to the charge that her writing is so difficult as to be inaccessible or elitist. "I do not think that in our societies, an intellectual's ultimate vocation is to create a social accord based on clarity, transparency and simplification," she says. "There are organizations and devices for that. On the contrary, it seems to me that if an intellectual has a reason to exist, it is in the single measure where he affirms and propagates a difference" (my translation).

2. See *Tales of Love* here, especially "God Is Love," where Kristeva considers the way in which the Christian understanding of love facilitates the construction of subject identity, how it, "favors my leap into the Name of the Father" (144). Significantly, in Christianity, as distinct from Judaism, love requires the death of the body, she says, the killing of the believer's body as condition for identification with the divine ideal. In Christianity, "love is the experience of becoming *homologous*," but there is no idealizing identification, no setting up of the believer as the subject of the Other, without the death of the lustful body: "The killing of the body is the path through which the body-Self has access to the Name of the Other who loves me and makes of me a Subject who is immersed (baptized) in the Name of the Other" (146).

3. The point is made by Derrida, Lyotard, and Lacan, as well as by Kristeva: the ethical subject does not precede the text as its author-owner. The subject does not *come before us*.

4. Kristeva's status as an "exile" has been both romanticized and overlooked. As an example of the former, see the remarks with which Jean-Paul Enthoven opens "Julia Kristeva: à quoi servent les intellectuels?": "First, there is her voice: serious, but with a Bulgarian accent that gives her students from Paris-VII the impression that they are not listening to a professor but to one of those actressses exiled from *l'entre-deux-guerres*. A delicacy, almost Chinese, with an insane, seductive smile. Her age: at least thirty-five. Finally, her name, that for her alone could have made for this recent emigrant from Eastern Europe a type of secret counsellor for melancholic intellectuals" (my translation). On the other hand, her status as an exile is overlooked by those "geophilosophers" who deal with her and her writing as, simply, "French," and as exemplifying "French feminism," or "French poststructuralism," or the "postmodernism" of "the French."

5. The writing subject, Kristeva says, is "a pulverized and shattered being. The individual, insofar as he is a speaking being, witnesses a permanent radical crisis, he is much less an entity—as one would believe through etymology than a contradictory constellation" (1977d, 98, my translation).

6. "I seized upon Saussure's *Anagrammes*, parts of which Jakobson and Starobinski had published. From this starting point, I tried to establish a 'paragrammatical' conception of the literary text as a distortion of signs and their structures that produces an infinitesimal overdetermination of meaning in literature" (1984c, 225).

7. That ethics is "heard" as "silent" suggests an "accord" with Lyotard here: with his "exhorbitant law" of a listening that cannot spare the one who listens "the despair of never hearing what the voice says" (1990, 22).

8. Kristeva (1983) stresses the need to read for the heterogeneous, the exhorbitant, in Lacan, "[t]o keep it unresolved" (36), not to reduce his language to signification.

9. In "Stabat Mater," Kristeva "assumes and glorifies, as only a Christian can, Freud's version of the traditional (modern) view of femininity as motherhood," Teresa de Lauretis maintains (1989, 269). According to Ann Rosalind Jones, Kristeva's positioning of women "outside the Symbolic" serves to reinforce the "long-term, mainstream tendency in Western thought to exclude women, along with madmen and slaves, from cultural centrality" (1984, 62). Along the same lines, see Kaja Silverman's critique of "Stabat Mater" (1988, 101–26).

10. Like Lacan, Kristeva suggests that fragmentation or division belongs to the child's "prehistory," and therefore that the *chora* (a term she uses to suggest a space or place "anterior" to language) does not imply an original unity, an idyllic and harmonious beginning outside of the Father's binary law. For this reason, the "before" of the *chora*, like that of Lacan's mirror stage, cannot simply be read into the before/after logic of a periodization, a developmental history, or a diachronic theory of language.

11. Abjection is different from "uncanniness" and more violent too, Kristeva says in *Powers of Horror* (5), for abjection—the jettisoning, the radical exclusion-expulsion of what is separate, other, not me, threatening to the I's identity, threatening to system and order, and so loathsome (2–4)—"is elaborated through a failure to recognize its kin." In abjection, she says, "nothing is familiar" (5). And yet, she

also says that abjection confronts us "with our earliest attempts to release the hold of the maternal entity" such that, under the law of the father, the mother "will turn into an abject," and abjection itself will become "*a precondition of narcissism*" (13). In the sections of *Powers of Horror* which examine the place of the mother in Céline's fiction, Kristeva explores further this relation between abjection and primary narcissism, and especially between abjection and the body of the birth-giving woman. See also her "Ellipsis on Terror and the Specular Seduction" (1979).

12. "As with any society, the countersociety is based on the expulsion of an excluded element, a scapegoat charged with the evil of which the community duly constituted can then purge itself; a purge which will finally exonerate that community of any future criticism. Modern protest movements have often reiterated this logic, locating the guilty one—in order to fend off criticism—in the foreign, in capital alone, in the other religion, in the other sex. Does not feminism become a kind of inverted sexism when this logic is followed to its conclusion?" (1981c, 27).

13. "This identification by women with the very power structures previously considered as frustrating, oppressive, or inaccessible has often been used in modern times by totalitarian regimes: the German National-Socialists and the Chilean junta are examples of this. The fact that this is a paranoid type of counterinvestment in an initially denied symbolic order can perhaps explain this troubling phenomenon; but an explanation does not prevent its massive propagation around the globe, perhaps in less dramatic forms than the totalitarian ones mentioned above, but all moving towards leveling, stabilization, conformism, at the cost of crushing exceptions, experiments, chance occurrences" (1989c, 26).

14. These third generation feminists would be engaged in the search for what Kristeva, in "Stabat Mater," calls "an heretical ethics, an *herethics*" (263), a contemporary ethics "no longer seen as being the same as morality" (262). Such an ethics, an ethics *after*, "after the Virgin" (262), would not, she says, avoid "the embarrassing and inevitable problematics of the law," but rather would seek to give the law "flesh, language, *jouissance*" (262). It would be a kind of "WORD FLESH" (235), situated on place of the wound or scar, the thetic boundary where "speech causes biology to show through" (263). The "wound" (see also Kristeva 1984c) suggests not only the physical, birth-giving rupture, but also the "tearing" of the subject at the

thetic boundary, as well as the scar of the trauma and triumph of the "battle with the Phallic Mother" ("The Novel as Polylogue," in 1980a, 193).

15. For Kristeva, as for Derrida, Lyotard, Lacan, and Foucault, the time of modernity (and so of postmodernity) is always in question. The time of modernity, we might say, is the time of patriarchal history, "time as project, linear and prospective unfolding; time as departure, progression, and arrival" (1981c, 17). The time of patriarchal history gives the order of language, "considered as the enunciation of sentences (noun + verb; topic-comment; beginning-ending)" (17). And according to Francis Bacon in his *Temporus partus masculus* (*The Masculine Birth of Time*), the linear succession of language coincides with the order of nature itself. From nature (defined in essentialist terms) derives, in turn, "the enlightened predictability of the world" and the task of putting into proper order as "the shape of the history to come" (Reiss 1982, 221).

16. Lyotard uses the word *cadere* in *Heidegger and "the jews"* (17), and like Kristeva, in a discussion of the fear and violence that are bound up with writing, and of the need, therefore, to "give space" to the subject.

17. *In the Beginnning Was Love: Psychoanalysis and Faith*, 7

5. Comings and Goings

1. One point I hope to demonstrate in this chapter is that Foucault uses both "text" and "discourse" in the widest sense of the terms. He does not restrict the former to the written or printed book on the shelf, nor the latter to oral speech, and he does not separate either from "the world."

2. It is from his "heroes" that Foucault takes his "renversed style," White claims. Foucault's "heroes" would be "the victims" (White, "Foucault's Discourse" 114) of power as well as a group of "mad" artists: "Foucault values the brilliant opacity, the dark superficiality, the casual profundity of those writers who inhabit the silent places left by the discourse of 'normal' men" (115).

3. For example, White suggests (1987, 117–20) that in *Madness and Civilization*, the modern discourse on madness is shown by Foucault to go through four phases between the Middle Ages and our own time. These four phases, White says, correspond to the fundamental

modes of figuration identified by the theory of tropes: metaphor, metonymy, synecdoche, and irony.

4. It would be as a repressive theory, as an account that gives us the truth (the hidden secret) of the subject, that Foucault opposes psychoanalysis. I am not able to take the matter up here, but there are affinities, I think, between Foucault's work and that of Lacan.

5. It is, of course, not only Foucault's book on Roussel that is folded. According to Foucault's understanding of language, every text is a woven tissue, constituted through multiple folds. Indeed, for Foucault, to use Maurice Blanchot's words, each linguistic element "is already multiple in itself, or, more precisely, it is a non-unitary multiplicity" (1987, 75).

6. See for example, H. J. Muller's argument (1950) which illustrates the idea of genetic load that caught on in both population and medical genetics. As a measure of reduced reproductive success or "impaired fitness," genetic load was linked to the adverse effects of technological innovation, including the progressive use of ionizing radiation and radioactive materials, but at the same time, the idea was used to support the proliferation of new technologies for monitoring and adminstering the public health. The concept of genetic load (burden) carried over from population genetics to medical genetics where, through genetic counseling, it became necessary to the argument that new reproductive controls are defences of the genetic health of the social body.

7. Foucault refers to this catachretic style in his introduction to *The Use of Pleasure*, in the context of discussing the "long detour" of his sexuality series occasioned by his turning back to Greek and Roman texts: "The risks? First, there was the likelihood of delaying and upsetting the publication schedule that I had projected. I am grateful to those who followed the advances and detours of my work—and I am thinking of my auditors at the Collège de France—and to those who had the patience to wait for its outcome—Pierre Nora in particular. As to those for whom to work hard, to begin and begin again, to attempt and be mistaken, to go back and rework everything from top to bottom, and still find reason to hesitate from one step to the next—as to those, in short, for whom to work in the midst of uncertainty and apprehension is tantamount to failure, all I can say is that clearly we are not from the same planet" (7).

8. See for example, the introduction to *Before Sexuality* by David Halperin, John Winkler, and Froma Zeitlin, eds., and in that volume, Peter Brown's "Bodies and Minds: Sexuality and Renunciation in Early Christianity." It is only after acknowledging Foucault's "rare perceptiveness" in *Le souci de soi* that Brown takes on "one of the most enduring misperceptions of European history": that Christianity only "rendered more coherent, more stringent because more internalized and truly 'spiritual,' codes of sexual discipline that had already been canvassed, in a less consequential manner, by the finest minds of paganism" (480).

Works Cited

Appiah, Anthony. 1986. "Deconstruction and the Philosophy of Language." *Diacritics* 16.1 (1986): 49–64.

Bacon, Francis. 1859. *Temporus Partus Masculus. The Works of Francis Bacon.* Vol. 3. Eds. James Spedding, Robert Leslie Ellis, and Douglas Heath. London: Longman.

Barthes, Roland. 1970. "L'Étrangère." *Quinzaine Littéraire.* 1–15 May, pp. 19–20.

Baudrillard, Jean. 1984. "The Precession of Simulacra." In *Art after Postmodernism,* ed. Brian Wallis. New York: The New Museum of Contemporary Art; Boston: David R. Godine, 253–281.

———. 1986. "The Year 2000 Will Not Take Place." In *Futur*Fall: Excursions into Post-Modernity,* eds. E. A. Grosz, Terry Threadgold, David Kelly, Alan Cholodenko, and Edward Colless. Sydney: Power Institute of Fine Arts, 18–28.

Bell, Rudolph. 1985. *Holy Anorexia.* Chicago: University of Chicago Press.

Bennington, Geoff. 1988. *Lyotard: Writing the Event.* New York: Columbia University Press.

Bennington, Geoff, and Robert Young. 1987. "Introduction: Posing the Question." In *Post-structuralism and the Question of History,* eds. Derek Attridge, Geoff Bennington, and Robert Young. Cambridge: Cambridge University Press, 1–11.

Bernard of Clairvaux. 1976. *The Works of Bernard of Clairvaux.* Vol. 3: *On the Song of Songs II.* Trans. Kilian Walsh. Kalamazoo: Cistercian Publications.

Bernasconi, Robert. 1987. "Deconstruction and the Possibility of Ethics." In *Deconstruction and Philosophy: The Texts of Jacques Derrida*, ed. John Sallis. Chicago: University of Chicago Press, 122–39.

Blanchot, Maurice. 1992. "Michel Foucault as I Imagine Him." In *Foucault/Blanchot*. Trans. Brian Massumi. New York: Zone.

Brodribb, Somer. 1992. *Nothing Matters: A Feminist Critique of Postmodernism*. North Melbourne: Spinifex.

Brown, Peter. 1990. "Bodies and Minds: Sexuality and Renunciation in Early Christianity." In *Before Sexuality: The Construction of Erotic Experience in the Ancient Greek World*, ed. David Halperin, John Winkler, and Froma Zeitlin. Princeton: Princeton University Press, 479–93.

Butler, Judith. 1993. "Sexual Inversions." In *Foucault and the Critique of Institutions*, ed. John Caputo and Mark Yount. University Park: Pennsylvania State University Press, 81–98.

Carroll, David. 1984. "Rephrasing The Political with Kant and Lyotard: From Aesthetic to Political Judgements." *Diacritics* 14.3 (1984): 74–88.

———. 1987. *Paraesthetics: Foucault, Lyotard, Derrida*. New York: Methuen.

———. 1990. "Foreword: The Memory of Devastation and the Responsibilities of Thought: 'And let's not talk about that'." Jean-François Lyotard, *Heidegger and "the jews."* Trans. Andreas Michel and Mark Roberts. Minneapolis: University of Minnesota Press, vii–xxix.

Caws, Mary Ann. 1973. "*Tel Quel*: Text and Revolution." *Diacritics* 3.1 (1973): 2–8.

Chadwick, Owen, ed. 1958. *The Sayings of the Fathers. Library of Christian Classics*, Vol. 13: *Western Asceticism*. London: SCM.

Clark, Michael. 1988. *Jacques Lacan: An Annotated Bibliography*. Vol. 1. New York: Garland.

Coward, Rosalind, and John Ellis. 1977. *Language and Materialism: Developments in Semiology and the Theory of the Subject*. Boston: Routledge.

Critchley, Simon. 1992. *The Ethics of Deconstruction: Derrida and Levinas*. Oxford: Blackwell.

de Certeau, Michel. 1986. *Heterologies: Discourse on the Other*. Trans. Brian Massumi. Minneapolis: University of Minnesota Press.

de Lauretis, Teresa. 1989. "The Female Body and Heterosexual Presumption." *Semiotica* 67.3–4 (1989): 259–79.

Deleuze, Gilles. 1986. *Foucault.* Trans. Seán Hand. Foreword by Paul Bové. Minneapolis: University of Minnesota Press.

Derrida, Jacques. 1974 *Of Grammatology.* Trans. Gayatri Spivak. Baltimore: Johns Hopkins University Press.

———. 1978a. "Coming into One's Own." In *Psychoanalysis and the Question of the Text,* trans. James Hulbert and ed. Geoffrey Hartman. Baltimore: Johns Hopkins University Press. 114–48.

———. 1978b. *Writing and Difference.* Trans. Alan Bass. Chicago: University of Chicago Press.

———. 1979. "Living On: Border-lines." In *Deconstruction and Criticism,* trans. J. Hulbert and ed. Harold Bloom et al. New York: Seabury. 75–176.

———. 1981a. "Economimesis." Trans. R. Klein. *Diacritics* (June 1981): 1–25.

———. 1981b. *Positions.* Trans. Alan Bass. Chicago: University of Chicago Press.

———. 1982a. *Margins of Philosophy.* Trans. Alan Bass. Chicago: University of Chicago Press.

———. 1982b. "Of an Apocalyptic Tone Recently Adopted in Philosophy." Trans. John Leavey. *Semeia* 23 (1982): 63–97.

———. 1983."*Geschlecht*: Sexual Difference, Ontological Difference." *Research in Phenomenology* 13 (1983): 65–83.

———. 1984a. "Deconstruction and the Other." In *Dialogues with Contemporary Continental Thinkers,* ed. Richard Kearney. Oxford: Manchester University Press, 107–26.

———. 1984b. "No Apocalypse, Not Now (full speed ahead, seven missiles, seven missives)." Trans. Catherine Porter and Philip Lewis. *Diacritics* 14 No. 2 (Summer 1984): 20–31.

———. 1984c. *Signéponge/Signsponge.* Trans. Richard Rand. New York: Columbia University Press.

———. 1985a. "Des Tours de Babel." *Difference in Translation,* trans. and ed. Joseph F. Graham. Ithaca: Cornell University Press. 165–207.

———. 1985b. *The Ear of the Other: Otobiography, Transference, Translation.* Trans. Peggy Kamuf. Ed. Christie McDonald. New York: Schocken.

———. 1986a. *Glas.* Trans. John Leavey and Richard Rand. Lincoln: University of Nebraska Press.

———. 1986b."Point de folie: Maintenant l'architecture." *AA Files* 12 (1986): 65–75.

———. 1986c. "Proverb: 'He that would pun . . .'." In *Glassary*, John Leavey. Lincoln: University of Nebraska Press, 17–20.

———. 1987a. "*Geschlecht* II: Heidegger's Hand." Trans. John P. Leavey, Jr. *Deconstruction and Philosophy: The Texts of Jacques Derrida*. Ed. John Sallis. Chicago: University of Chicago Press, 161–96.

———. 1987b. *The Post Card: From Socrates to Freud and Beyond*. Trans. Alan Bass. Chicago: University of Chicago Press.

———. 1987c. "Women in the Beehive: A Seminar with Jacques Derrida." In *Men in Feminism*, ed. Alice Jardine and Paul Smith. London: Methuen. 189–203.

———. 1988a. "An Interview with Jacques Derrida." In *Derrida and Différance*, ed. David Wood and Robert Bernasconi. Evanston: Northwestern University Press, 71–82.

———. 1988b. "Letter to a Japanese Friend." In *Derrida and Différance*, trans. David Wood and Andrew Benjamin and ed. David Wood and Robert Bernasconi. Evanston: Northwestern University Press, 1–5.

———. 1988c. *Limited INC*. Evanston: Northwestern University Press.

———. 1989a. "How to Avoid Speaking: Denials." In *Languages of the Unsayable: The Play of Negativity in Literature and Literary Theory*, trans. Ken Frieden and ed. Sanford Budick and Wolfgang Iser. New York: Columbia University Press, 3–70.

———. 1989b. *Of Spirit: Heidegger and the Question*. Trans. Geoffrey Bennington and Rachel Bowlby. Chicago and London: University of Chicago Press.

———. 1990. "Some Statements and Truisms about Neologisms, Newisms, Postisms, Parasitisms, and Other Small Seismisms." In *The States of 'Theory': History, Art, and Critical Discourse*, trans. Anne Tomiche and ed. David Carroll. New York: Columbia University Press, 63–111.

———. 1991. "At This Very Moment in This Work Here I Am." In *Re-Reading Levinas*, trans. Simon Critchley and ed. Robert Bernasconi and Simon Critchley. Bloomington: Indiana University Press, 11–48.

———. 1992a. "Force of Law: The 'Mystical Foundation of Authority'." In *Deconstruction and the Possibility of Justice*, trans. Mary Quaintance and ed. Drucilla Cornell, Michel Rosenfeld, and David Gray Carlson. New York: Routledge, 3–67.

————. 1992b. *Given Time: 1. Counterfeit Money.* Trans. Peggy Kamuf. Chicago: University of Chicago Press.

————. 1992c. "Passions: 'An Oblique Offering'." *Derrida: A Critical Reader.* Trans. and ed. David Wood. Oxford: Blackwell, 5–35.

————. 1993. "Heidegger's Ear: Philopolemology (*Geschlecht* IV)." Trans. John P. Leavey, Jr. *Reading Heidegger: Commemorations,* ed. John Sallis. Bloomington: Indiana University Press, 163–218.

During, Simon. 1992. *Foucault and Literature: Towards a Genealogy of Writing.* London: Routledge.

Engelhardt, H. Tristram. 1983. "Viability and the Use of the Fetus." In *Abortion and the Status of the Fetus,* ed. William Bondeson, H. T. Engelhardt, Stuart Spicker, and Daniel Winship. Dordrecht: D. Reidel, 183–208.

Eribon, Didier. 1991. *Michel Foucault.* Trans. Betsy Wing. Cambridge, Mass.: Harvard University Press.

Fenves, Peter, ed. 1993. *Raising the Tone of Philosophy: Late Essays by Immanuel Kant, Transformative Critique by Jacques Derrida.* Baltimore: Johns Hopkins University Press.

Finas, Lucette, Sarah Kofman, Roger LaPorte, and J.-M. Rey, eds. 1973. *Écarts: Quatre essais à propos de Jacques Derrida.* Paris: Fayard.

Forrester, John. 1984. "Freud, Dora and the Untold Pleasures of Psychoanalysis." In *Desire,* ed. Lisa Appiganesi. London: Institute of Contemporary Arts, 4–9.

Foucault, Michel. 1970. *The Order of Things: An Archaelogy of the Human Sciences.* Trans. unidentified collective. London: Tavistock.

————. 1990. *The History of Sexuality,* vol. 1: *An Introduction.* Trans. Robert Hurley. New York: Vintage.

————. 1977a. *Discipline and Punish: The Birth of the Prison.* Trans. Alan Sheridan. Harmondsworth: Penguin.

————. 1977b. "Nietzsche, Genealogy, History." *Language, Counter-Memory, Practice: Selected Essays and Interviews by Michel Foucault.* Ed. Donald F. Bouchard. Trans. Donald F. Bouchard and Sherry Simon. Ithaca: Cornell University Press, 139–64.

————. 1980 "The Confession of the Flesh." *Power/Knowledge: Selected Interviews and Other Writings 1972–1977.* Ed. Colin Gordon. New York: Pantheon, 194–228.

————. 1983. "On the Genealogy of Morals: An Overview of Work in Progress." In *Michel Foucault: Beyond Structuralism and Hermen-*

eutics. 2nd ed. With an Afterword by and an Interview with Michel Foucault. Ed. Hubert L. Dreyfus and Paul Rabinow. Chicago: University of Chicago Press, 229–52.

———. 1985. *The Use of Pleasure. The History of Sexuality*, vol. 2. Trans. Robert Hurley, New York: Vintage.

———. 1986. *Death and the Labyrinth: The World of Raymond Roussel*. Trans. Charles Ruas. Berkeley: University of California Press.

———. 1987. "Questions of Method: An Interview with Michel Foucault." In *After Philosophy: End or Transformation?*, ed. James Bohman and Thomas McCarthy. Cambridge: MIT Press, 100–117.

———. 1988a. "Critical Theory/Intellectual History." *Michel Foucault: Politics, Philosophy, Culture: Interviews and Other Writings 1977–1984*. Ed. Lawrence Kritzman. Trans. Alan Sheridan et al. London: Routledge, 17–46.

———. 1988b. *The Care of the Self. The History of Sexuality*, vol. 3. Trans. Robert Hurley. New York: Pantheon.

———. 1988c. "The Return of Morality." *Michel Foucault: Politics, Philosophy, Culture: Interviews and Other Writings 1977–1984*. Ed. Lawrence Kritzman. Trans. Alan Sheridan et al. London: Routledge, 242–54.

———. 1989a. "Clarifications on the Question of Power." *Foucault Live (Interviews, 1966–84)*. Trans. John Johnston. Ed. Sylvère Lotringer. New York: Semiotext(e), 179–92.

———. 1989b. "The Concern For Truth." *Foucault Live (Interviews, 1966–84)*. Trans. John Johnston. Ed. Sylvère Lotringer. New York: Semiotext(e), 293–308.

———. 1989c. "The Masked Philosopher." *Foucault Live (Interviews, 1966–84)*. Trans. John Johnston. Ed. Sylvère Lotringer. New York: Semiotext(e), 193–202.

Freud, Sigmund. 1970. *Letters 1873–1939*. Ed. Ernst L. Freud. London: Hogarth Press.

Gallop, Jane. 1982. *The Daughter's Seduction: Feminism and Psychoanalysis*. Ithaca: Cornell University Press.

Hadewijch d'Anvers. 1980. *The Complete Works*. Trans. Mother Columba Hart. New York: Paulist Press.

Halperin, David, John Winkler, and Froma Zeitlin, eds. 1990. *Before Sexuality: The Construction of Erotic Experience in the Ancient Greek World*. Princeton: Princeton University Press.

Hassan, Ihab. 1974. *The Dismemberment of Orpheus.* New York: Oxford University Press.

———. 1980. "The question of postmodernism." In *Romanticism, Modernism, Postmodernism,* ed. Harry R. Garvin. Lewisberg: Bucknell University Press, 117–26.

———. 1986. "Pluralism in postmodern perspective." *Critical Inquiry* 12.3 (1986): 503–20.

Heath, Stephen. 1977. "Translator's Note." Roland Barthes, *Image Music Text.* New York: Hill and Wang.

———. "Difference." *Screen* 19 (1978): 51–112.

Henriques, Julian, Wendy Holloway, Cathy Unwin, Couze Venn, and Valerie Walkerdine, eds. *Changing the Subject: Psychology, Social Relations and Subjectivity.* London: Methuen.

Howe, Elizabeth Teresa. 1988. *Mystical Imagery: Santa Teresa de Jesús and San Juan de la Cruz.* New York: Peter Lang.

Howey, Richard L. 1985. "Nietzsche and the 'New' French Philosophers." *International Studies in Philosophy* 17 (1985): 83–93.

Hutcheon, Linda. 1988a. *A Poetics of Postmodernism: History, Theory, Fiction.* New York: Routledge.

———. 1988b. "A Postmodern Problematics." In *Ethics/Aesthetics: Post-Modern Positions,* ed. Robert Merrill. Washington, D.C.: Maissonneuve Press, 1–10.

———. 1989 *The Politics of Postmodernism,* London: Routledge.

———. 1991. Afterword. In *Remembering Postmodernism: Trends in Recent Canadian Art,* ed. Mark A Cheetham and Linda Hutcheon. Toronto: University of Toronto Press, 109–29.

Huyssen, Andreas. 1986. *After the Great Divide: Modernism, Mass Culture, Postmodernism.* Bloomington: Indiana University Press.

Irigaray, Luce. 1985. *This Sex Which Is Not One.* Trans. Catherine Porter with Carolyn Burke. Ithaca: Cornell University Press.

Jacobus of Voragine. 1969. *Golden Legend.* Trans. Ryan Granger and Helmut Riggerger. New York: Arno.

Jameson, Fredric. 1971. *Marxism and Form: Twentieth-Century Dialectical Theories of Literature.* Princeton: Princeton University Press.

———. 1972. *The Prison House of Language: A Critical Account of Structuralism and Russian Formalism.* Princeton: Princeton University Press.

———. 1981. *The Political Unconscious: Narrative as Socially Symbolic Act.* Ithaca: Cornell University Press.

————. 1982. Interview. *Diacritics* 12.3 (1982): 72–91.

————. 1983. "Postmodernism and Consumer Society." *The Anti-Aesthetic: Essays on Postmodern Culture,* ed. Hal Foster. Port Townsend, Wash.: Bay Press, 111–25.

————. 1984. Foreword. Jean-François Lyotard, *The Postmodern Condition: A Report on Knowledge.* Trans. Geoff Bennington and Brian Massumi. Minneapolis: University of Minnesota Press, vii–xxi.

————. 1984a. "The Politics of Theory: Ideological Positions in the Postmodernism Debate." *New German Critique* 33 (1984): 53–65.

————. 1984b. "Postmodernism, or the Cultural Logic of Late Capitalism." *New Left Review* 146 (1984): 53–92.

————. 1987. "Regarding Postmodernism—A Conversation with Fredric Jameson." Interview by Anders Stephanson. *Social Text* 17 (1987): 29–54.

————. 1988a. *The Ideologies of Theory: Essays 1971–1986,* vol. 1: *Situations of Theory.* Minneapolis: University of Minnesota Press.

————. 1988b. *The Ideologies of Theory,* vol. 2: *Syntax of History.* Minneapolis: University of Minnesota Press.

————. 1990. "Spatial Equivalents: Postmodern Architecture and the World System." In *The States of 'Theory,* ed. David Carroll. 1990. 125–48.

Jardine, Alice. 1985. *Gynesis: Configurations of Woman and Modernity.* Ithaca: Cornell University Pres.

John of the Cross. 1964. *The Collected Works of John of the Cross.* Trans. Kieran Kavanaugh and Otilio Rodriguez. New York: Doubleday.

Johnson, Christopher. 1988. "Intertextuality and the Psychical Model." *Paragraph* 11.1 (1988): 11–89.

Jones, Ann Rosalind. 1984. "Julia Kristeva on Femininity: The Limits of a Semiotic Politics." *Feminist Review* 18 (1984): 56–73.

————. 1985. "Inscribing Femininity: French Theories of the Feminine." In *Making a Difference: Feminist Literary Criticism,* ed. Gayle Greene and Coppélia Kahn. London: Methuen. 80–112.

Kant, Immanuel. [1796] 1958. "Von einem neuerdings erhobenen vornehmen Ton in der Philosophie." *Schriften zur Metaphysik und Logik,* vol. 3. Wiesbaden: Insel-Verlag, 1958. 377–97. French translation: "D'un ton grand seigneur adopté naguère en philosophie." Trans. I. Guillermit. *Première introduction à la critique de la faculté de juger.* Paris: Vrin, 1975, 86–109.

———. [1798] 1974. *Anthropology from a Pragmatic Point of View.* Trans. Mary Gregor. The Hague: Martinus Nijhoff.

———. [1790] 1978. *The Critique of Judgement.* Trans. James Creed Meredith. Oxford: Clarendon.

Kearney, Richard. 1987a. "Ethics and the Postmodern Imagination." *Thought* 62, 244 (1987): 39–58.

———. 1987b. "The Crisis of the Postmodern Image." In *Contemporary French Philosophy,* ed. A. Phillips Griffiths. Cambridge: Cambridge University Press. 113–22.

Kraus, Henry. 1967. *The Living Theatre of Medieval Art.* Philadelphia: University of Pennsylvania Press.

Kristeva, Julia. 1969. *Séméiótiké: Recherches pour une sémanalyse.* Paris: Seuil.

———. 1973. "The Ruin of a Poetics." In *Russian Formalism,* ed. Stephen Bann and Joseph Boldt. Edinburgh: Scottish Academic Press, 102–19.

———. 1974. "Phonetics, Phonology and Impulsional Bases." Trans. Caren Greenberg. *Diacritics* 4.3 (1974): 33–37.

———. 1977a. "Modern Theatre Does Not Take (A) Place." Trans. Alice Jardine and Thomas Gora. *Sub-Stance* 18–19 (1977): 131–34.

———. 1977b. *Polylogue.* Paris: Seuil.

———. 1977c. "Un nouveau type d'intellectuel: le dissident." *Tel Quel* 74 (1977): 3–8.

———. 1977d. "Julia Kristeva: à quoi servent les intellectuels?" Interview by Jean-Paul Enthoven. *Le Nouvel Observateur* 77 (June): 97–136.

———. 1979. "Ellipsis on Terror and the Specular Seduction." Trans. Dolores Burdick. *Wide Angle* 3.2 (1979): 42–47.

———. 1980a. *Desire in Language: A Semiotic Approach to Literature and Art.* Ed. Leon Roudiez. Trans. Thomas Gora, Alice Jardine, and Leon Roudiez. New York: Columbia University Press.

———. 1980b. "Postmodernism?" In *Romanticism, Modernism, Postmodernism,* ed. Harry R. Garvin. Lewisberg: Bucknell University Press, 136–41.

———. 1981a. "La femme, ce n'est pas jamais ça." In *New French Feminisms.* Trans. Marilyn August. Ed. Elaine Marks and Isabelle de Courtivron. New York: Schocken, 136–41.

———. 1981b. "Oscillation du 'pouvoir' au 'refus'." *New French Feminisms*. Trans. Marilyn August. Eds. Elaine Marks and Isabelle de Courtivron. New York: Schocken, 165–67.

———. 1981c. "Women's Time." Trans. Alice Jardine and Harry Blake. *Signs* 7.1 (1981): 13–35.

———. 1982. *Powers of Horror: An Essay on Abjection*. Trans. Leon Roudiez. New York: Columbia University Press.

———. 1983. "Within the Microcosm of 'The Talking Cure'." In *Interpreting Lacan*, ed. Joseph Smith and William Kerrigan. New Haven: Yale University Press, 33–48.

———. 1984a. "An Interview with Julia Kristeva." By Perry Meisel. *Partisan Review* 51.1 (1984): 128–32.

———. 1984b. "Julia Kristeva in Conversation with Rosalind Coward." *Desire*. Ed. Victor Burgin, Rosalind Coward, John Forrester, Rosemary Gordon, Mary Kelly, Julia Kristeva, Toril Moi, Laura Mulvey, Kathy Myers, and Riccardo Steiner. London: Institute of Contemporary Arts Documents, 22–27.

———. 1984c. "My Memory's Hyperbole." In *The Female Autograph*. Trans. Athena Viscusi. Ed. Domna Stanton. Chicago: University of Chicago Press, 219–35.

———. 1984d. *Revolution in Poetic Language*. Trans. Margaret Waller. New York: Columbia University Press.

———. 1987a. *In the Beginning Was Love: Psychoanalysis and Faith*. Trans. Arthur Goldhammer. New York: Columbia University Press.

———. 1987b. *Tales of Love*. Trans. Leon Roudiez. New York: Columbia University Press.

———. 1989a. *Black Sun: Depression and Melancholy*. Trans. Leon Roudiez. New York: Columbia University Press.

———. 1989b. *Language the Unknown: An Initiation into Linguistics*. Trans. Anne M. Menke. New York: Columbia University Press.

———. 1991. *Strangers to Ourselves*. Trans. Leon Roudiez. New York: Columbia University Press.

Kroker, Arthur and David Cook. 1986. *The Postmodern Scene: Excremental Culture and Hyper-Aesthetics*. Montréal: New World Perspectives.

———. 1987. "Panic Sex in America." In *Body Invaders: Panic Sex in America*, ed. Kroker and Kroker. Montréal: New World Perspectives, 10–34.

Kroker, Arthur and Kroker, Marilouise. 1985. "Preface: the Phallocentric Mood: 'Bored but Hyper'." In *Feminism Now: Theory and Practice,* ed. Arthur and Marilouise Kroker, Pamela McCallum, and Mair Verthuny. Montréal: New World Perspectives, 5–6.

Kroker, Arthur. 1984. *Technology and the Canadian Mind: Innis/McLuhan/ Grant.* Montréal: New World Perspectives.

———. 1987. "Panic Value: Bacon, Colville, Baudrillard and the aesthetics of deprivation." In *Life after Postmodernism: Essays on Value and Culture,* ed. Richard Fekete. Montréal: New World Perspectives, 181–93.

———. 1992. *The Possessed Individual: Technology and the French Postmodern.* Montréal: New World Perspectives.

Lacan, Jacques. 1968. *Speech and Language in Psychoanalysis.* Trans. Anthony Wilden. Baltimore: Johns Hopkins University Press.

———. 1975. *Le Séminaire livre XX, Encore.* Ed. Jacques-Alain Miller. Paris: Seuil.

———. 1977a. *Écrits: A Selection.* Trans. Alan Sheridan. New York: Norton.

———. 1977b. *The Four Fundamental Concepts of Psychoanalysis.* Trans. Alan Sheridan. New York: Norton.

———. 1986. *L'éthique de la psychanalyse: Seminar VII (1959–60).* Ed. Jacques-Alain Miller. Paris: Seuil.

———. 1988a. *The Seminar of Jacques Lacan,* book I: *Freud's Papers on Technique (1953–54).* Ed. Jacques-Alain Miller. Trans. John Forrester. New York: W. W. Norton.

———. 1988b. *The Seminar of Jacques Lacan,* book II: *The Ego in Freud's Theory and in the Technique of Psychoanalysis (1954–55).* Ed. Jacques-Alain Miller. Trans. Sylvana Tomaselli. New York: W. W. Norton.

Lacoue-Labarthe, Philippe, and Jean-Luc Nancy, eds. 1981. *Les fins de l'homme: à partir du travail de Jacques Derrida.* Paris: Editions Galiée.

Laurentin, R. 1968. *Court traité sur la Vierge Marie.* 5th ed. Paris: Lethielleux.

Levinas, Emmanuel. 1991. "Wholly Otherwise." In *Re-Reading Levinas.* Trans. Simon Critchley. Ed. Robert Bernasconi and Simon Critchley. Bloomington: Indiana University Press, 3–10.

Lewis, Philip. 1974. "Revolutionary Semiotics." *Diacritics* 4.3 (1974): 28–32.

Lincoln, Victoria. 1984. *Teresa: A Woman*. Albany: SUNY Press.

Lyotard, Jean-François, and Jean-Loup Thébaud. 1985. *Just Gaming*. Trans. Wlad Godzich. Minneapolis: University of Minnesota Press.

Lyotard, Jean-François. 1981. "Discussions, ou: phraser 'après Auschwitz'." In *Les fins de l'homme: à partir du travail de Jacques Derrida*, ed. Philippe Lacoue-Labarthe and Jean-Luc Nancy. Paris: Éditions Galilée, 283–315.

————. 1984. *The Postmodern Condition: A Report on Knowledge*. Trans. Geoff Bennington and Brian Massumi. Minneapolis: University of Minnesota Press.

————. 1988a. *The Differend: Phrases in Dispute*. Trans. Georges van den Abbeele. Minneapolis: University of Minnesota Press.

————. 1988b. *Peregrinations: Law, Form, Event*. New York: Columbia University Press.

————. 1989. "Anamnesis of the Visible, or Candour." *The Lyotard Reader*. Ed. Andrew Benjamin. Oxford: Blackwell 220–39.

————. 1990. *Heidegger and "the jews"*. Trans. Andreas Michel and Mark Roberts. Minneapolis: University of Minnesota Press.

————. 1991a. "Sensus Communis: The Subject in *Statu Nascendi*." In *Who Comes after the Subject?*, ed. Eduardo Cadava, Peter Connor, and Jean-Luc Nancy. New York: Routledge, 217–35.

————. 1991b. *The Inhuman: Reflections on Time*. Trans. Geoffrey Bennington and Rachel Bowlby. Stanford: Stanford University Press.

————. 1992. *The Postmodern Explained: Correspondence 1982–1985*. Trans. Don Barry, Bernadette Maher, Julian Pefanis, Virginia Spate, and Morgan Thomas. Minneapolis: University of Minnesota Press.

————. 1993. *Political Writings*. Trans. Bill Readings and Kevin Paul. Minneapolis: University of Minnesota Press.

MacIntyre, Alasdair. 1980. "A crisis in Moral Philosophy: Why is the Search for Foundations of Ethics so Frustrating?" In *Knowing and Valuing: The Search for Common Roots*, ed. H. Tristram Engelhardt and Daniel Callahan. New York: The Hastings Center, 18–35.

————. 1981. *After Virtue: A Study in Moral Theory*. Notre Dame, Ind.: University of Notre Dame Press.

————. 1988. *Whose Justice? Which Rationality?* Notre Dame, Ind.: University of Notre Dame Press.

————. 1990. *Three Rival Versions of Moral Inquiry: Encyclopaedia, Genealogy, and Tradition*. Notre Dame, Ind.: University of Notre Dame Press.

Mitchell, Juliet and Rose, Jacqueline, eds. 1982. *Feminine Sexuality: Jacques Lacan and the École Freudienne*. New York: W. W. Norton.

Moi, Toril. 1986. Introduction. *The Kristeva Reader*. Ed. Toril Moi. New York: Columbia University Press, 1–22.

Muller, H. J. 1950. "Our Load of Mutations." *American Journal of Human Genetics* 2.2 (1950): 111–76.

Nancy, Jean-Luc. 1992. "Elliptical Sense." In *Derrida: A Critical Reader*, trans. Peter Connor and ed. David Wood. Oxford: Blackwell, 36–51.

Owens, Craig. 1983. "The Discourse of Others: Feminists and Postmodernism." In *The Anti-Aesthetic: Essays on Postmodern Culture*, ed. Hal Foster. Port Townsend, Wash.: Bay Press, 57–82.

Patton, Paul. 1986. "Ethics and Post-Modernity." In *Futur*Fall: Excursions into Post-Modernity*, ed. E. A. Grosz, Terry Threadgold, David Kelly, Alan Cholodenko, and Edward Colless. Sydney: Power Institute of Fine Arts, 128–45.

Ragland-Sullivan, Ellie. 1987. *Jacques Lacan and the Philosophy of Psychoanalysis*. Urbana: University of Illinois Press.

Ragusa, Isa, and Rosalie Green, eds. 1961. *Meditations on the Life of Christ*. Trans. Isa Ragusa. Princeton: Princeton University Press.

Reiss, Timothy. 1982. *The Discourse of Modernism*. Ithaca: Cornell University Press.

Rose, Jacqueline. 1982. Introduction II. *Feminine Sexuality: Jacques Lacan and the École Freudienne*, ed. Juliet Mitchell and Jacqueline Rose. New York: W. W. Norton, 27–57.

Roudiez, Leon. 1974. "Twelve Points from *Tel Quel*." *Esprit Createur* 14.4 (1974): 291–303.

Schulenburg, Jane Tibbetts. 1986. "The Heroics of Virginity: Brides of Christ and Sacrifical Mutilation." In *Women in the Middle Ages and the Renaissance: Literary and Historical Perspectives*, ed. Mary Beth Rose. Syracuse: Syracuse University Press, 29–72.

Sciascia, Leonardo. 1972. *Actes relatifs à la mort de Raymond Roussel*. Paris: L'Herne.

Siebers, Tobin. 1986. "The Ethical Unconscious." *The Psychoanalytic Review* 73.3 (Fall 1986): 309–31.

Silverman, Kaja. 1988. *The Acoustic Mirror: The Female Voice in Psychoanalysis and Cinema*. Bloomington: Indiana University Press.

Slemon, Stephen. 1990. "Modernism's Last Post." In *Past the Last Post*, ed. Ian Adam and Helen Tiffin. Calgary: University of Calgary Press, 1–11.

Spanos, William. 1987. *Repetitions: The Postmodern Occasion in Literature and Culture*. Baton Rouge: Louisiana State University Press.

Spivak, Gayatri Chakravorty. 1977. "*Glas*-Piece: A Compte Rendu." *Diacritics* 6.3 (Fall 1977): 22–43.

———. 1984. "Love Me, Love My Ombre, Elle." *Diacritics* 14.4 (Winter 1984): 19–36.

Stanton, Domna C. 1984. Preface. In *The Female Autograph*, ed. Domna Stanton. Chicago: University of Chicago Press, vii–xi.

Stewart, Garrett. 1990. *Reading Voices: Literature and the Phonotext*. Berkeley: University of California Press.

Suleiman, Susan Rubin. 1991. "Feminism and Postmodernism: A Question of Politics." In *Zeitgeist in Babel: The Postmodernist Controversy*, ed. Ingeborg Hoesterey. Bloomington: Indiana University Press, 111–30.

Teresa of Avila. 1946. *The Complete Works of Saint Teresa of Jesus*, vol. 3. Trans. E. Allison Peers. London: Sheed & Ward.

———. 1957. *The Complete Works of Saint Teresa of Jesus*, vol. 1. Trans. E. Alison Peers. London: Sheed & Ward.

———. 1980. *The Collected Works of St. Teresa of Avila*. Trans. Kieran Kavanaugh and Otilio Rodriguez. Washington, D.C.: ICS Publications.

———. 1989. *The Interior Castle*. Trans. E. Allison Peers. New York: Doubleday.

Underhill, Evelyn. 1955. *Mysticism*. Chicago: Meridian.

von Hildebrand, Dietrich. 1962. *In Defense of Purity: An Analysis of the Catholic Ideals of Purity and Virginity*. Baltimore: Helicon Press.

Walker, Barbara. 1983. *The Woman's Encyclopedia of Myths and Secrets*. San Francisco: Harper & Row.

Weber, Samuel. 1991. *Return to Freud: Jacques Lacan's Dislocation of Psychoanalysis*. Trans. Michael Levine. Cambridge: Cambridge University Press.

White, Hayden. 1987. "Foucault's Discourse: The Historiography of Anti-Humanism." In *The Content of the Form: Narrative Discourse and Historical Representations*. Baltimore: Johns Hopkins University Press, 104–41.

Wilden, Anthony. 1968. "Translator's Introduction" and "Lacan and the Discourse of the Other." In Jacques Lacan, *Speech and Language in Psychoanalysis*. Baltimore: Johns Hopkins University Press, vii–xix, 159–311.

Zepp, Evelyn H. 1982. "The Criticism of Julia Kristeva: A New Mode of Critical Thought." *Romantic Review* 73.1 (1982): 80–97.

Index